The
Night Sky
Revealed

The Night Sky Revealed

MARTIN RATCLIFFE

Star Charts by
CHARLES NIX

BARNES
&NOBLE
NEW YORK

ACKNOWLEDGMENTS

Martin Ratcliffe: This publication would not have been possible
without the thoughtful guidance, calm editorship, and keen
insight of George Scott, who led this project to completion with
consummate skill and a steady hand. This guide owes its design to
the creative skills of Charles Nix. To both of you, thank you. Rich
Talcott of *Astronomy* magazine helped with proof reading. Thanks
Rich for lending your skills to yet another project. Any errors that
remain, of course, are mine to own. Thanks to the entire Barnes
& Noble team for your enthusiasm for this project, and skillfully
taking it through to publication. My enduring love and thanks to
my two girls, Victoria and Emma, who, during the writing of this
guide, created many colorful drawings while I wrote. Thanks to
Kate for your friendship. Thanks to my outstanding local support
team. Each of you knows how valuable your encouragement,
inspiration, friendship, and support were to me during this special
project, and you know who you are. Finally thanks to my friends
in the world of planetariums, and in my native United Kingdom
and Ireland where my family and friends in various astronomical
societies gave me such a good start. I am eternally grateful.
Finally, thanks to you, the reader of this guide. I truly hope it opens
up the wonders of the universe for you.

Scott & Nix: Scott & Nix extend their thanks to the publishing
team at Barnes & Noble, Nathaniel Marunas, Michael Vagnetti,
and Ruth O'Brien. We also thank the many amateur and
professional astrophotographers who contributed images,
especially Dennis C. Anderson, Adam Block, Ronald Dantowitz,
Fred "MrEclipse.com" Espenak, Tony and Daphne Hallas, Damian
Peach, and John Sanford.

PREPARED BY
SCOTT & NIX, INC.
150 WEST 28TH STREET, SUITE 1103
NEW YORK, NY 10001

WE WELCOME YOUR QUESTIONS AND COMMENTS ABOUT THIS PRODUCT.
PLEASE SEND THEM VIA E-MAIL TO NIGHTSKY@SCOTTANDNIX.COM

GEORGE SCOTT, EDITOR
CHARLES NIX, ART DIRECTOR
RICH TALCOTT, CONSULTING EDITOR

ISBN-13: 978-0-7607-9327-5
ISBN-10: 0-7607-9327-1

PRINTED IN CHINA

10 9 8 7 6 5 4 3 2 1

STAR CLUSTERS IN ANTENNAE GALAXIES (NASA, ESA, AND HUBBLE HERITAGE TEAM)

FRONTISPIECE: GALAXIES IN CLUSTER ABELL 50740 (NASA, ESA, AND HUBBLE HERITAGE TEAM)
PAGE VI: STARBURST GALAXY—M82 (NASA, ESA, AND HUBBLE HERITAGE TEAM)

Contents

STAR-FORMING REGION IN THE LARGE MAGELLANIC CLOUD (NASA, ESA, AND HUBBLE HERITAGE TEAM)

Introduction to the Universe

*T*he Night Sky Revealed is the perfect reference to begin exploring the universe from your own backyard. With simple instructions on how to follow the revolution of the night sky throughout the year and amazing facts about, and astonishing images of, the objects in the night sky, this book is your key to begin unlocking the mysteries of the heavens. This book is divided into four major sections: Introduction to the Universe, Practical Astronomy, The Solar System, and The Year of the Night Sky.

• The Introduction to the Universe explores the fascinating features of our universe, such as the various types of galaxies, the life of a star, black holes, solar systems, and observable phenomena including meteor showers, comets, and auroras.

• The Practical Astronomy section contains everything you need to know about using the night sky charts in the book along with brief explanations of basic astronomical concepts.

• The Solar System section reveals in separate chapters the secrets of the planets in our solar system, plus the Moon and Sun. Each chapter contains detailed information about observing objects in the solar system including advice on optimum times and dates for best viewings.

• The Year of the Night Sky section guides you through a year of astronomical observation. Each month has two side-by-side charts that show all the major constellations, stars, and deep-sky objects. The apparent night sky chart on the left uses glow-in-the-dark ink to mimic the appearance of the actual night sky. The quadrant chart on the right has even more details about the night sky including ranks of magnitude and types of visible objects. For the entire year, clearly written text and vital tips are included that describe the heavenly highlights of the months, tables for the constellations, the brightest stars, and the most prominent deep-sky objects.

May *The Night Sky Revealed* foster a lifelong interest in the stars. Clear skies!

THE UNIVERSE

The universe is expanding. We've all heard this statement in various contexts, but what does it mean exactly? The simple answer is that every distant galaxy appears to be moving away from us. The more distant galaxies appear to be moving faster. From measuring the rate of this expansion and other factors, scientists have determined that all the stuff that makes up the universe was once densely packed together in an area perhaps no bigger than an atom. For reasons unknown, 13.7 billion years ago, this tiny area expanded rapidly in an instant known as the Big Bang.

Within one second after the Big Bang, energy in the form of subatomic particles and radiation cooked together at astoundingly hot temperatures. After three minutes, the ultra-hot subatomic particles came together as nuclei. The universe then cooled for about 300,000 years and when the hot fog lifted, the universe became transparent and filled with energy in the form of light and stable atoms. Over the next 300 million years, clumps of matter and energy formed hot stars, quasars, and early galaxies. It took several billion years from the instant of the Big Bang for our home galaxy, the Milky Way, to form, and then 4.6 billion years ago, our solar system was formed.

The Big Bang "theory" has stood the test of time since first proposed by cosmologists. Year after year since the late 1920s, experiments and careful scientific studies have shown that all evidence points to the Big Bang as the best model for the creation of the universe.

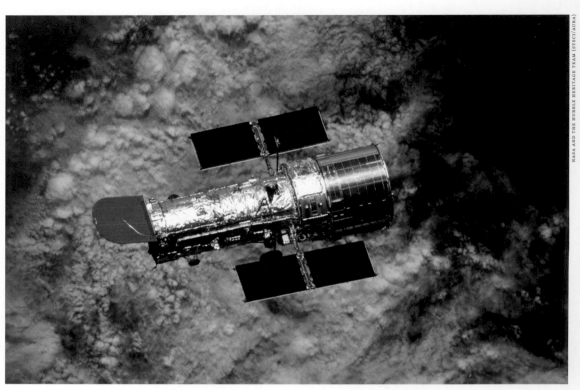

In the 1920s, the American astronomer Edwin Hubble discovered that the more distant a galaxy is from us, the faster it appears to be moving away. This discovery laid the foundation for modern cosmology, the study of the origins and destiny of the universe. In honor of Hubble, NASA named its famous orbiting telescope after the first modern cosmologist.

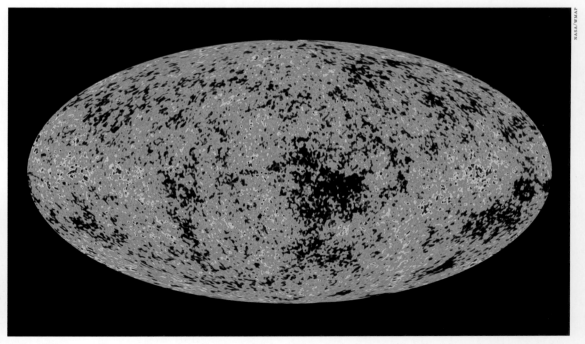

The Wilkinson Microwave Anisotropy Probe is shown here in an artist's view on its way to an orbiting position 1 million miles from Earth. After looping the Earth three times, it flew by the Moon's orbit to catch some gravitational energy for its long journey.

In the 1960s, two radio astronomers, Arno Penzias and Robert Wilson, picked up what they thought was interference in their new microwave antenna. After studying it carefully, they discovered that it was, in fact, cosmic microwave background radiation—leftover energy from the creation of the universe. In 2001, NASA launched the Wilkinson Microwave Anisotropy Probe into orbit to measure minute fluctuations in the cosmic microwave background radiation. Data from the probe was used to create this image, which represents the oldest light in the universe. Study of this data allowed scientists to give 13.7 billion years as the age of the universe.

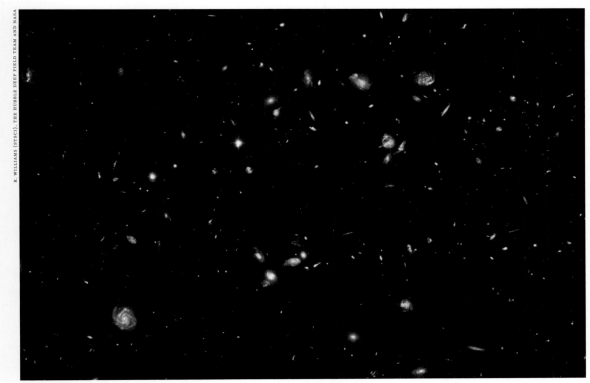

R. WILLIAMS (STSCI), THE HUBBLE DEEP FIELD TEAM AND NASA

GALAXIES

Galaxies are enormous congregations of stars, "star cities," and some contain gas, dust, and other cosmic debris. Galaxies are varied in shape, from featureless ellipticals to highly structured spirals. Ellipticals are older, whereas spirals contain many areas of new star formation, such as those found in our own Milky Way.

We see the stars in the Milky Way, our home galaxy, from the inside. The Milky Way is made up of different spiral arms and contains an estimated 150 billion stars. Our galaxy is immense. It takes light, traveling at 186,000 miles per second (6 trillion miles per year), 100,000 years to cross the Milky Way from one side to the other. The Earth lies about 30,000 light years from the center, so about a third of the way out. From our line of sight on Earth, we view some distant galaxies as tilted, such as the Andromeda galaxy, or face on, such as the Whirlpool galaxy.

The Hubble Space Telescope took this amazing image over ten days looking farther into space than ever before. The "ultra-deep field" image caused a sensation because it revealed thousands of new galaxies never seen before, some perhaps 12 billion light years from Earth. There is one star in this image. Every other object is a galaxy.

ADAM BLOCK/NOAO/AURA/NSF

NASA AND THE HUBBLE HERITAGE TEAM (STSCI/AURA)

ADAM BLOCK/NOAO/AURA/NSF

The nearest galaxy similar to our Milky Way is the Andromeda galaxy, about 2.7 million light years away. Both are huge spiral galaxies. From Earth, many spirals have different shapes because of the angle of our perspective. When viewed edge-on, the dusty spiral arms bisect the bright core.

Spiral galaxies, such as the Whirlpool galaxy shown here, contain gas, dust, old stars, and newly formed stars. The older stars are yellow in color and congregate near the core of galaxies. Hot young blue stars are found in spiral arms, associated with clouds of gas and dust.

Elliptical galaxies contain old generations of stars that have used up all the gas and debris that once surrounded them. M87 is shown here complete with its bright jet of material emanating from its core.

LIFE OF A STAR

Neighboring stars are too far away to reveal many details to us on Earth. However, we can measure their brightness, distance, and composition with remarkable accuracy. Decades of research have led to a clear picture of the formation and evolution of stars.

A star begins within a cocoon of gas and dust, inside one of the huge nebulae that populate the spiral arms of galaxies. Denser regions within a nebula slowly contract under their own gravitation. The center of the contracting cloud begins to heat up and rotate faster. This rotation forces the gas into a disk around the central contracting core.

Once the temperature in the center of the cloud reaches about 10 million degrees, thermonuclear fusion reactions begin. Hydrogen is fused into Helium and massive amounts of energy are released. A star is born.

A star reaches the late stages of its life when the mass of helium in its core reaches more than 10 percent of the star's mass. The energy being generated is no longer enough to support its own weight. From this point onwards, the star begins a cycle that will ultimately lead to its demise. The core shrinks, temperature rises, and higher temperature fusion reactions occur. The outer envelope of the star expands to become a red giant.

Stars less than one-and-a-half times the mass of our Sun will begin a slow contraction, and perhaps in some stellar version of indigestion, suddenly erupt, ejecting a shell of gas that produces a planetary nebula. The core of the star slowly fades to become a white dwarf star.

More massive stars go through a much more dramatic ending. The star becomes a red supergiant, much larger than its giant relatives. Once the fusion reactions form iron in the core, no further energy generation is possible. The end of the star is abrupt. The core collapses under its own weight in less than a second. A huge shockwave rips through the outer layers of the supergiant,

This fantastic image of the Eagle Nebula from the Hubble Space Telescope shows the birthplace of stars inside billowing clouds of glowing hydrogen gas and dust. The central tower is 9.5 light-years high (about 57 trillion miles).

NASA, ESA, AND THE HUBBLE HERITAGE TEAM (STSCI/AURA)

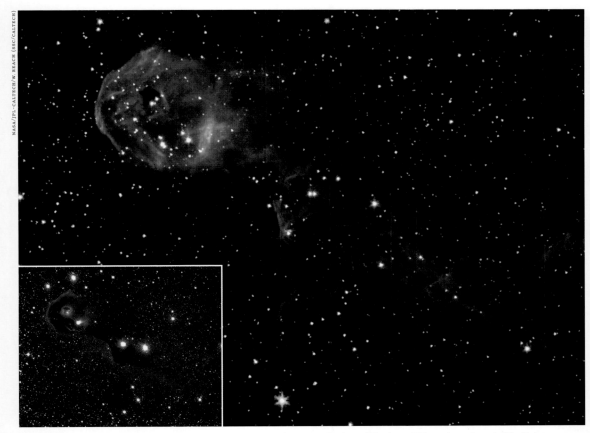

NASA/JPL-CALTECH/W. REACH (SSC/CALTECH)

The Elephant's Trunk Nebula is 2,450 light years away in the constellation of Cepheus. When viewed at visible-light wavelengths (inset) starlight appears trapped within the nebula. The infrared view by the Spitzer Space Telescope (large image) penetrates the dust to reveal unseen young stars forming inside the dark cocoon.

erupting all the remaining gas in a stupendous nuclear fireball called a supernova. The light generated by such a cataclysm can outshine an entire galaxy. It's within such explosions that all elements in the universe that are heavier than iron are formed. The explosion seeds the interstellar medium with heavy elements, ready for a future generation of stars to form, perhaps with planets orbiting them.

The core of the star becomes an incredibly compact object called a neutron star. These rapidly rotating objects have intensely strong magnetic fields generating huge energy that is able to light up the expanding nebula. The prime example of such an object is the Crab Nebula. The orginal star exploded over 900 years ago, and is still expanding. It contains the first ever identified rotating neutron star, also called a pulsar, named for its rapid series of radio pulses.

More massive stars will create an even more massive object as they collapse. The atomic nuclei are crushed beyond existence into a black hole, where the density is infinitely high and gravity is strong enough to prevent light escaping from a region of space a few miles across.

SOLAR SYSTEMS

Planetary systems are known to form around stars within huge clouds of gas and dust. These stellar nurseries contain dozens of objects that have stars buried within donut-shaped cocoons of dust and gas. As a star forms, the cooler gas and dust orbit in a thin disk.

Denser regions of the disk begin accumulating material, growing in size. The largest objects grow faster and eventually carve out gaps within the dusty disk.

The growing planetoids—they are not fully-fledged planets yet—are impacted by millions of tons of floating debris in the disk. Gradually the disk is cleared out, leaving a group of planets orbiting a star.

The eight major planets of our solar system and Pluto are pictured here in a composite image shown to relative scale, not to relative distance from the Sun. The four gas giants, Jupiter, Saturn, Uranus, and Neptune, dwarf the other rocky planets by a large magnitude. With the exceptions of Mercury and Venus, all the planets have at least one orbiting moon. Jupiter has the most with 63 moons identified to date. The minor planets are part of a large asteroid belt between Mars and Jupiter and are thought to be leftover material from the formation of the major planets.

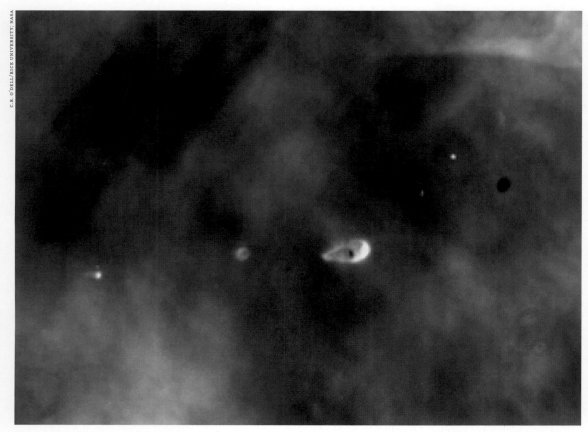

Proplyds are clumpy proto-planets forming from dust and other space debris. The Hubble Space Telescope took this image of a small section within the Orion Nebula, a "nursery" of many new stars. The four orange stars in the image are new stars surrounded by gas and dust. Scientists think this may be a "baby picture" of a new solar system.

In 1997, Comet Hale-Bopp was seen by more people than any other comet in history. It was the brightest comet since Comet West appeared in the night sky 21 years earlier in 1976. Scientists studying images made by the Hubble Space Telescope determined that the nucleus of Hale-Bopp to be approximately 25 miles in diameter.

Our early solar system was a place of tremendous change. As the dusty and rocky disk of material coalesced, the newly forming planets would run into other objects in their path. The evidence of these early impacts are scattered across every planet and moon in the form of craters.

The Hubble Space Telescope has provided unprecedented views of young stars with debris disks around them. This combination of previous theory and direct observation is a key component toward the understanding of how our planetary system formed.

Our solar system consists of eight planets, over 100 natural satellites or moons, asteroids, and comets. Each planet has a unique appearance. The inner four planets are dense, rocky, relatively small objects. Beyond the orbit of Mars, four giant planets, made primarily of hydrogen and helium, orbit the Sun in the cold dark reaches of the solar system. Beyond Neptune lies a region called the Kuiper Belt that is filled with icy bodies left over from the early formation of our solar system. Occasionally one of these icy rocks, known as Kuiper Belt objects, swings toward the Sun and becomes visible as a comet. A few larger Kuiper Belt objects have names, such as Sedna and Quaoar. Two dwarf planets are also found in the belt, Eris and Pluto (once considered a full planet).

COMETS, ASTEROIDS, METEORS

On any moonless, dark night, there is a good chance that after 10 or 15 minutes you will spot the brief streak of light across the sky called a meteor. They are caused by tiny particles of dust, or tiny pebbles of rock, striking the atmosphere at an average speed of 40 miles per second. At this speed, the vaporization of the particle is instantaneous and gives off light.

Meteors and comets are related in an interesting way. As a comet orbits the Sun, the evaporating ices and ejected dust become deposited behind it. These particles continue orbiting the Sun long after the comet has visited the inner solar system. If the path crosses Earth's orbit, then at the same time of the year the Earth will run into the stream of particles. Those that strike the atmosphere will burn up as a

Meteors appear to radiate from one point in the sky and are associated with particular constellations. This time-lapse image shows the Leonid showers associated with the constellation Leo.

ANNUAL METEOR SHOWERS

SHOWER	DATES	PEAK	APPROX. NO. PER HR.
Quadrantids	Jan 1–6	Jan 3	100
Lyrids	Apr 19–25	Apr 22	10
Eta Aquarids	Apr 24–May 20	May 4	40
Perseids	Jul 23–Aug 20	Aug 12	80
Orionids	Oct 16–27	Oct 20	25
Leonids	Nov 15–20	Nov 17	20
Geminids	Dec 7–16	Dec 13	100

meteor. Before the particle, or rock, reaches the atmosphere, it is called a meteoroid. A meteor is actually the vapor trail of the meteoroid as it burns up. If the original meteoroid is large enough to survive entry into the atmosphere, it can land on Earth and becomes a meteorite.

Typically on any clear, moonless night, you can see on average about seven meteors per hour. When Earth crosses the orbit of a comet, this rate increases. They produce regular annual showers, since the orbit remains relatively fixed in space, so the Earth encounters them on roughly the same date every year.

Some comets, such as Tempel-Tuttle, have left significant clumps of material along its orbit. While it is rare for the Earth to encounter this trail of dust, when it does, a meteor storm results. The Temple-Tuttle comet is linked to the Leonid meteor shower, and significant storms resulted in over hundreds, and in certain locations, thousands, of meteors per hour in 1999, 2001, and 2002. The Orionid meteor shower is associated with the most famous comet of all, Halley's comet.

Typically more meteors are seen after midnight. Before midnight, our view is backwards along our orbit, where the Earth has just been. If meteors are coming from this direction they have to catch up with us. After midnight, we are facing in the same direction as the motion of the Earth. Meteors from this direction strike our atmosphere head on and the intensity of their trail will be brighter. In the hour or so before dawn, our direction of flight is highest in the sky. During major showers, such as the Perseids and Leonids,

Comet tails always point directly away from the Sun. Like a pebble in a stream, comets sit in a high-speed stream of particles from the Sun called the solar wind. In one part of the orbit, the appearance is of the comet moving "backwards," or tail first, along its orbit.

The European space probe Giotto flew within 370 miles of Halley's Comet in March 1986. It transmitted the first detailed image of a comet's nucleus ever seen.

keep a watch even as twilight grows. Often the most intense fireballs have been observed at this time. A fireball is classed as a meteor that shines brighter than Venus.

Comets are dirty snowballs that spend most of their lives in a dormant state far from the Sun.

When charged particles from the Sun strike the Earth's magnetic field, they light up the particles present in our atmosphere and discharge energy in the form of light. The beautiful colors are caused by the particles reacting to elements in the thermosphere (50 miles up).

They are made of ice and dust, presumably pristine material from the early formation of the solar system that has remained untouched. It is for this reason that comets attract so much attention from scientists.

Occasionally a comet will venture into the inner solar system. Solar radiation causes the ices to sublime (turning from solid to gas). As the comet flies along its orbit, a huge gas cloud envelops the solid nucleus. When viewing from Earth, the nucleus is not visible, but the gas cloud, called a coma, is. Most comets remain this way, and appear as small fuzzy spots in the sky, changing position from night to night.

Bright comets are very rare. During the 1990s two bright comets appeared within a year of one another. In 1996, Comet Hyakutake appeared (top left image), passing within 9 million miles of Earth. It became bright because of its closeness to the Earth, and its faint tail, only seen from dark locations, extended well over half the sky.

In 1997, comet Hale-Bopp was one of the largest and brightest comets seen in modern times. Halley's comet is the most famous, though not the brightest. Its last return to the inner solar system occurred in 1986. It won't be seen again until 2061.

AURORAS

Most frequently seen at high latitudes, observers may be treated to the beautiful phenomenon of aurora borealis (northern hemisphere) and aurora australis (southern hemisphere). This shimmering of multicolored light occurs when charged particles trapped in the Earth's magnetic field accelerate and strike the gasses in our atmosphere. Solar winds flow over the Earth's magnetic field and power these energetic particles.

Practical Astronomy

Looking up at the night sky, we see light from billions and trillions of miles away. Some of this light began traveling to us long before the formation of the Earth, solar system, and our own galaxy, and is just reaching our planet now. This light may be gone in an instant, once it reaches Earth, or may persist for as long as the universe continues to exist. Some light shines with amazing regularity for us to enjoy each evening. Throughout the years of our life, faraway galaxies and nebulae glow faintly, planets from the solar system shine brightly, the constellations flow across the sky throughout the seasons, and our Moon waxes and wanes. Watching the night sky can be as simple as appreciating the twinkle of a distant star on a summer's evening, and luckily, there is a nearly infinite number of objects to appreciate year after year.

The Night Sky Revealed is meant as a primer to amateur astronomy. Each section has practical advice about observing the night sky, diagrams, facts about objects, and tables of annual and upcoming astronomical events. There are many useful books that go into great detail and will be of use should you decide to learn more about the night sky. Many web sites provide good, reliable information about astronomy and space exploration. A brief list of resources along with a glossary of terms is included at the end of this book.

USING THE MONTHLY CHARTS

The Year of the Night Sky section features two charts to the night sky for each month of the year. A chart of the apparent night sky approximates the arrangement of the major constellations by joining stars into their classical shapes and shows the location of major deep-sky objects. The individual stars on this chart are printed with luminous ink that may be charged with incandescent or fluorescent light. After several minutes of exposure, the charts will glow in the dark for some time, and will help you make out the shapes of the constellations indoors or out.

The quadrant chart on the facing page is a detailed map with constellation boundaries and individual stars labeled by rank of magnitude. The brightest stars are of the 1st magnitude and the very faintest stars visible to the naked eye are of the 6th magnitude. The individual stars that make up a constellation are also given ranks in Greek letters from alpha (usually the brightest) to omega (dimmest). For example,

Sirius, is "alpha" in the constellation Canis Major. For reference, a table of the Greek alphabet is included with each month's chart.

MAGNITUDES

● ● ● • · ·
Sirius 1 2 3 4 5

The magnitude scale in the charts is used to provide a guide to the brightness of each star. Some objects, such as Sirius (mag. −1.5), appear with the largest dot.

The chart also includes the location of the major deep-sky objects. This chart is not printed with luminous ink and will be most useful when using binoculars or a telescope when you are out stargazing.

The relative sizes of the stars on both charts depict the stellar brightness by degree of magnitude. A medium-powered telescope will see down to about magnitude +13. The Hubble Space Telescope can reach to about magnitude 30. At the brighter end of the scale,

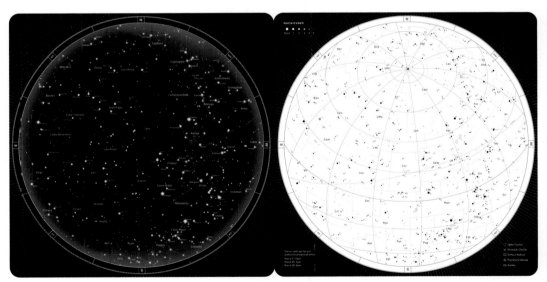

Both charts show the entire sky of the northern hemisphere. Imagine the night sky above you is a dome and the charts in the folders as flattened versions of the dome. The outer edge of each chart represents the horizon and the center of each chart is the location directly overhead, called the zenith. When using the charts, determine which direction you are facing and place the cardinal point of your chart at the bottom. For example, if you are facing west, rotate the chart so that the map is oriented to the western horizon.

some objects in the sky are brighter than the first-magnitude, so the scale is extended to magnitude 0, then to negative numbers, −1, −2 and so on.

Venus typically shines at magnitude −4. The full Moon is magnitude −12.5, and the Sun is magnitude −26.8. The human eye is capable of discerning a brightness difference between stars of one-tenth of a magnitude. Digital detectors can measure a star's brilliance to one-hundredth, or even one-thousandth of a magnitude.

The stars on the charts in this book are shown down to magnitude +4.5. The stars are printed in relative scale with the brightest stars larger than fainter ones. A few night's experience of using the charts will quickly make you familiar with the magnitude scale.

The most difficult aspect of learning the constellations for the first time is recognizing the size of each group. Remember that on your chart, the short distance from the horizon to its center equates to a wide expanse of sky from the real horizon to a point high overhead.

Form an imaginary line across each star chart from north to south running through the zenith; this is called the meridian. When facing south, stars to the left of the meridian are east, and those to the right are west. A star rises in altitude in the eastern sky and reaches a maximum when it reaches the meridian, lying precisely due south. Each location on Earth has its own unique meridian. A telescope located on the Prime Meridian of the world, in Greenwich, England, was used to define the zero point for longitude measurement on Earth.

Times listed on the charts are for local time, with daylight saving time (DST) adjusted for the period from early April to late October. The listed times should be treated as a general guide for the rising and setting of the constellations and planets. The charts represent a particular time for roughly the middle of the United States and depending on where you live, rising and setting times may differ slightly.

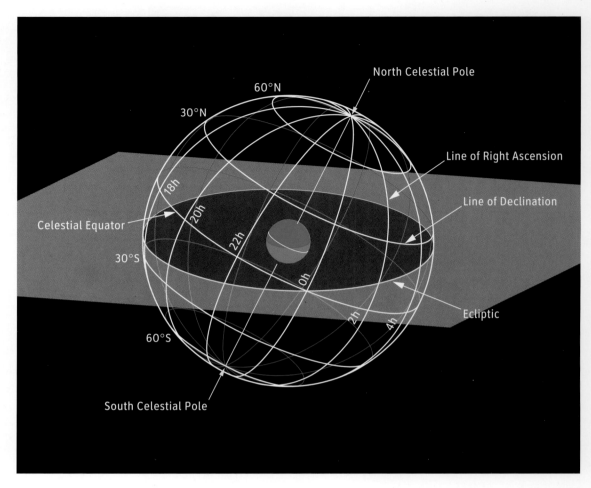

THE CELESTIAL SPHERE

Locating objects in the sky is a little more complicated than longitude and latitude on Earth. However, it's easy to imagine a sphere surrounding the Earth with a grid that matches the lines of latitude and longitude. This is the celestial sphere. It has two poles, each lying directly above the North and South Pole of the Earth. It has an equator, a giant circle spanning the entire sky much like the equator of the Earth. From any point on the Earth's surface, the viewer sees half of the celestial sphere at one time. The angle above and

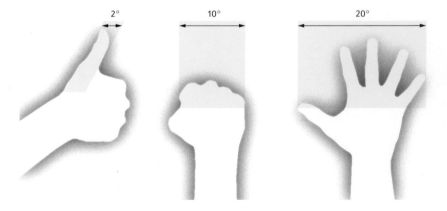

A quick and easy way to measure degrees of altitude in the night sky is by using your outstretched arm. Hold your arm straight out towards the sky. An average open hand measures about 20° from thumb to pinky finger. A closed fist measures 10° and a thumb equals about 2°.

This composite satellite image of the entire Earth at night clearly shows high population centers. Electric lights from cities, factories, airports, streetlights, and homes light up the night sky in many places, obscuring all but the brightest stars and planets. Some communities shield electric lights at night to help reduce "light pollution" for better stargazing.

below the equator is called declination. It ranges from 0° at the equator to +90° at the North Pole and −90° at the South Pole.

Longitude has an equivalent in charting the sky called right ascension (sometimes abbreviated R.A.). While longitude on Earth is measured in degrees, right ascension is measured in elapsed time since the zero point crosses your local meridian. This is a line that runs north to south through the zenith. On Earth, the zero point of longitude is the Greenwich Meridian. In the sky, the zero point is where the Sun's path across the celestial sphere crosses the celestial equator. This occurs in two places, so the one occurring in spring is arbitrarily selected as the zero point. The entire celestial sphere is divided into 24 hours, so one hour is equivalent to a 15° angle in the sky. The right ascension of an object is determined by measuring the time it takes after the zero point crosses the meridian until the object does so.

TIME

The rotation of the Earth gives us day and night, and the rotation rate defines the length of the day. The Earth orbits the Sun along an elliptical orbit, and when we are closer to the Sun, the Earth moves along its orbit faster than when farther away. Since the Earth rotates at constant speed, the Sun gets ahead or behind during the average 24-hour period. The difference in the length of the day as measured by the Sun is between 14 to 16 minutes. A smoothing out of this variation is done by an imaginary Mean Sun, and gives us our Mean Solar Time, or the 24-hour day. The period of rotation of the Earth itself is shorter relative to the stars, at 23h 56m 4.09s. This is called the sidereal day.

CONSTELLATIONS AND THE ZODIAC

Some of the familiar names of the constellations, such as Taurus and Leo, date back many thousands of years, and various cultures through the

centuries have created their own versions. For early observers, connecting the stars into a shape was an easy way to remember them, aside from any spiritual aspect they might have had. It was also a matter of practicality for early navigation and general direction.

Today there are 88 constellations that astronomers recognize for reference when plotting and observing the night sky. The charts in this book include 37 of the constellations viewable from the northern hemisphere. The Sun passes through 13 constellations along the ecliptic, and 12 of them are the basis for the signs of the zodiac.

VIEWING DEEP-SKY OBJECTS

With a few exceptions, most of the deep-sky objects on the charts will not jump out at you. While a magnitude may be listed as near naked eye at magnitude 6, sometimes that light is spread out over a large area, making the actual object

TELESCOPES

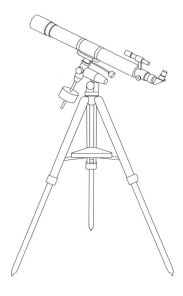

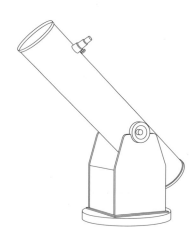

A refractor is the most familiar type of telescope and it is also the most expensive. Four lens surfaces are made to exacting specifications for quality refractors. They are excellent for planetary and lunar observations because they give high-contrast images. This telescope is shown mounted on an altazimuth mount. To track an object across the sky as it moves, this mount needs to be moved in both axes.

A refractor with a more expensive equatorial mount will allow accurate tracking of celestial objects. This mount has one fixed axis aligned to the Earth's polar axis and a second perpendicular axis that rotates to follow the sky. Take special care in selecting the correct mount for your telescope. If your telescope is too heavy for a mount, it will never provide a stable platform for observing the sky.

The Newtonian reflector is the most economical telescope because only one reflecting surface is required. An open tube with a mirror at the lower end reflects light up the tube to a small secondary mirror angled at 45° to reflect the image to the side of the tube. The most basic type of mount is the Dobsonian (shown here), a simple altazimuth (two axis) mount. Some Dobsonians have computerized pointing capabilities.

The Schmidt-Cassegrain is a combination lens and mirror in a closed tube and is a good quality, general purpose telescope. Some have mounts with sophisticated controls, including "Go To" capability. A handset with positions of thousands of celestial objects controls the orientation. Following careful set-up, such telescopes can almost eliminate the long periods of searching for faint objects. A computer with software can control some mounts. With a click of a mouse, the telescope will slew (move) to a desired object.

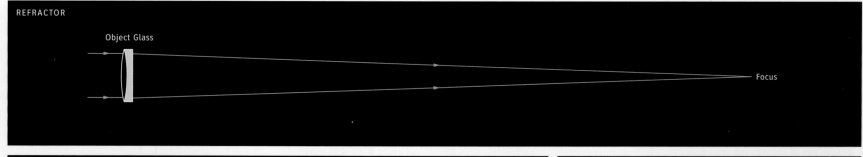

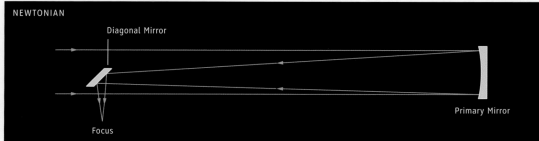

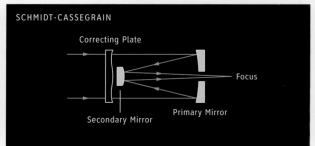

Refractor (top) — light passes through the lens and is focused. An eyepiece then magnifies the image. Newtonian Reflector (left) — light travels down the tube, reflecting off a parabolic mirror, back up the tube to a small mirror set at a diagonal. This reflects the light through the side of the tube to an eyepiece. Schmidt-Cassegrain (right) — light enters the tube by passing through a thin meniscus lens, strikes a spherical mirror, returns to a secondary mirror mounted on the inside of the meniscus lens, and is directed through a hole in the primary mirror.

very difficult to see. Magnification of your telescope also affects the visibility of deep-sky objects. High magnification is not the way to go. Usually low magnification is best. Binoculars often give the best view of some objects, such as the Pleiades and Hyades in Taurus.

VIEWING THE NIGHT SKY

Seeing. Earth's atmosphere is quite turbulent, especially after a warm day. Long after the Sun has set, the upper atmosphere contains bubbles of warm rising air and cool descending air. This turbulence plays havoc with the starlight, causing it to twinkle.

In addition, a telescope removed from a warm space to the cool night air will experience internal turbulence for at least 30 minutes, rendering poor quality images of the planets and Moon. Leave your telescope set up for at least 30 minutes before using it for the best views.

Transparency. Dust in the atmosphere diminishes the intensity of starlight reaching us from the night sky. Even at best, stars appear three magnitudes fainter near the horizon than overhead. During daytime, if the sky is a milky blue color, the transparency is poor. A deep blue sky indicates very good transparency, a foreteller of a good night to go galaxy hunting. However, good transparency does not guarantee good seeing.

Light Pollution. Local or citywide street lighting shines upwards where it is unwanted, creating the familiar glow across the sky that causes fainter stars and the Milky Way to be hidden from view. Specialized filters can remove some of the effects for photographic purposes, but the casual viewer of the sky has little recourse unless dark skies are within an easy drive. Some cities have light ordinances that require full-cut-off lighting fixtures. These fixtures can significantly reduce pollution of the night sky, and have two added benefits of reducing glare and requiring less energy than regular streetlights to illuminate the ground.

Telescopes. Owning a good telescope is the dream of many an aspiring amateur astronomer. It is important to point out that the images used in most astronomical books, including this one, and in magazines, show the planets, stars, and galaxies in color after long time exposures. The eye is incapable of seeing these details. Our eyes don't accumulate light over long periods of time like a sensitive digital sensor (CCD) or photographic film. So be wary of all advertising for telescopes—they assume you know the images shown are not those seen through a telescope, but those recorded by experienced astronomical photographers under ideal conditions.

However, the view of the Moon, Jupiter, and Saturn through your own telescope is breathtaking. One of the first rules for choosing a telescope is: magnification does not matter, light gathering power does. Choose a telescope based on its aperture (lens or mirror diameter). High magnification also magnifies the imperfections in a telescope's optics, and in the atmospheric turbulence above. Typically low or medium magnifications work best. A good rule of thumb is to use a magnification no higher than 50 times per inch of aperture. For a 60 mm refractor, the limit would be about $100 \times$. Eyepieces offering higher magnification than this are virtually useless, except for the highest quality and most expensive telescopes.

Magnification. Different eyepieces provide different magnification for telescopes. Three eyepieces provide a good start for the new observer: one giving low power (wide field of view), medium power, and high power (for use under the best sky conditions). Magnification can be determined by dividing the focal length of the telescope by the focal length of the eyepiece. For example, a telescope with 2000 mm focal length and a 25 mm eyepiece will produce a magnification of 80 times. Note that this is regardless of the diameter of the lens or mirror.

Solar Filters. Full aperture solar filters are a necessity for safe viewing of the Sun through any type of telescope. Looking through an unfiltered

or improperly filtered telescope of any kind will cause blindness. The filter should have paperwork that defines it as safe for viewing the Sun. Even so, never take this for granted, and check the filter for pinholes. Such defects render a filter useless. Never gamble with your eyesight by using a damaged filter.

Night Vision. Your eyes are remarkably adaptable to seeing in the dark, but they need to be given time to adjust. It will take your eyes at least 10 minutes, and preferably half an hour, to become accustomed to the dark sky. Avoid looking at any stray light and in particular any glare from bright lights. Any blue, white or green light will immediately destroy your night vision. Try to use only red light, such as the LED flashlight in this kit, because it has a minimal effect on your night vision.

Binoculars. Binoculars are very useful for viewing comets and wider swaths of sky. Mounting binoculars on a tripod gives the best views. Binocular sizes are given by their lens diameter and magnification. A pair of 7×50s has a magnification of seven times and a pair of lenses each 50 mm across. A pair of 10×50s is probably the largest possible to hold steady in your hands. Larger binoculars become too heavy to hold for any length of time. Binoculars will show craters and mountains on the Moon and many deep-sky star clusters and nebulae.

IMAGING THE NIGHT SKY

Today's modern digital cameras are capable of taking excellent photographs of the night sky. Each contains a charge-coupled device (CCD), an electronic detector capable of recording light. Digital cameras are rapidly replacing film as the medium of choice for astronomical photographers.

All photography through telescopes, either with digital or film cameras, requires an accurately aligned equatorial mount that tracks the object being photographed. The required accuracy of alignment increases with increasing exposure times. Computer-controlled altazimuth telescopes will reveal rotation of the field of view in time exposures. Field de-rotators are available.

INFANT STARS IN THE SMALL MAGELLANIC CLOUD (NASA, ESA, AND A. NOTA)

Digital Cameras. The most basic digital cameras can obtain photographs of the Moon by simply holding the lens to the eyepiece of a telescope. Digital camera adapters are available for mid-range and high-end digital cameras. When combined with specially designed eyepieces, a combination of camera lens and eyepiece generates high magnification for photography of the planets, Sun, and Moon. The lens-eyepiece combination is called "afocal" photography.

The most expensive digital cameras are the single-lens reflex (SLR) variety. Like their film-based predecessors, these can be fitted with suitable adapters and used on the telescope. The telescope effectively becomes a very large telephoto lens.

Webcams. Webcams can be hooked up to a telescope using an adapter that fits the telescope in place of an eyepiece. Video can be recorded through a USB port on a computer. Because video records 30 frames per second, the turbulence in the atmosphere is frozen in each image. Software, some of it freely available (for example, Registax and Astrostack), will take the randomly variable noise caused by turbulence in an image and remove it, leaving the surface detail of a planet visible. This detail can then be image processed to enhance contrast. Such techniques have revolutionized planetary photograph for the amateur.

CCD Cameras. These specialized astronomical cameras carry cooled CCD chips that are highly sensitive to light. These expensive cameras require a computer to operate, and each camera comes with its own proprietary software control package. First used by professional astronomers, a number of companies offer advanced CCD cameras to the amateur astronomer. The highest end cameras exceed 11 megapixels, and easily compete with film for quality and resolution.

Film. Photographic film is still used by many experienced astrophotographers, though its use is diminishing rapidly. Less expensive and more powerful CCD chips become available each year.

The Sun

OBSERVING THE SUN

After taking some simple precautions, monitoring sunspots and recording other features of our central star is one of the most satisfying pursuits in astronomy. There is constant change in the Sun's appearance, numerous occasions for surprise, and the occasional sunspot that breaks records.

The safest way to observe the Sun is to project its image onto a white card mounted behind the eyepiece of a telescope. After adjusting the focus, the Sun's disk and some of its features will appear almost magically on the card.

Align your telescope to the Sun without looking through it—don't ever attempt to sight along the telescope near the eyepiece.

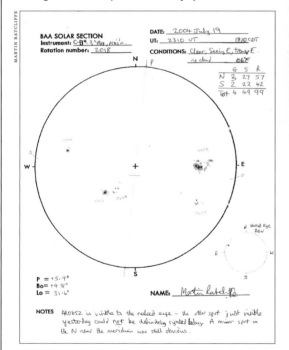

CAUTION: NEVER LOOK AT THE SUN USING A TELESCOPE WITHOUT A SAFE, CERTIFIED FILTER SYSTEM. SUNLIGHT IS EXTREMELY POWERFUL AND WILL BURN THE RETINA OF YOUR EYE RESULTING IN BLINDNESS. ALWAYS PLACE YOUR SOLAR FILTER AT THE FRONT OF THE TELESCOPE. FILTERS FOR TELESCOPE EYEPIECES ARE TOO DANGEROUS AND MAY SHATTER UNDER THE INTENSE HEAT OF THE MAGNIFIED SUN.

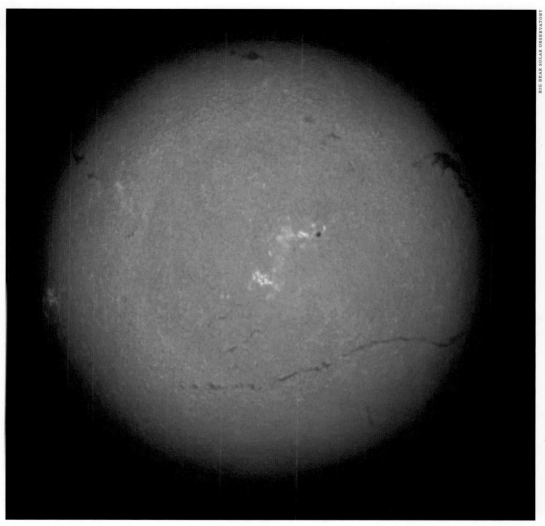

Above: This image of the Sun was captured using a Hydrogen Alpha filter fixed to the aperture end of a telescope. Used properly, the filter allows direct observation of the Sun without risk of injury to eyesight and will reveal many features otherwise obscured by its powerful rays. Left: Projecting an image of the Sun from a telescope allows observers to record sunspots and other prominent features.

Look at the shadow of the telescope on the ground. If the scope is not pointing directly at the Sun, the shadow of the telescope tube will appear elongated. Swivel the telescope on its mount, pointing the aperture to the Sun until the shadow of the tube itself is at its smallest. This means you've aligned the telescope's aperture properly to project the Sun directly through the eyepiece. With small adjustments, you will see the bright flash of sunlight projected onto your card. Don't use binoculars this way. The Sun's rays will cause adhesives in the lens mounting

to dissolve and will permanently damage your binos—save them for stargazing at night.

Daily drawings of the Sun will allow you to determine the longitude and latitude of sunspots if you have the correct orientation for your drawing. The Sun's rotation axis is tilted by 7.25° and the Earth's axial tilt is 23.5°. Simply align your grid to the east-west drift of sunspots seen on the projected disk. You'll need the latitude and longitude of the center of the Sun's disk for the date of your observation. The Astronomical Almanac, published by the US Naval Observatory, and its web site, can provide you with this "heliographic" data.

Looking directly through a telescope to observe the Sun should only be attempted when using specially designed solar filters. Reputable manufacturers make them to exacting specifications. The filters should be full aperture-types that mount very securely to the front end of your telescope. With this setup you can make finely detailed drawings of sunspots and take photographs.

Filters designed to select the light of hydrogen in the red part of the spectrum are widely available. These filters reveal spectacular prominences, at any time of the year. Solar prominences change shape, sometimes within minutes, and occasionally giant arching prominences will be in view. Filaments, the name given to prominences that are backlit by the solar disk, frequently appear around active regions on the Sun as dark fingers of gas.

SUNSPOTS

Sunspots are regions of intense magnetic activity that restrict the outflow of heat from beneath the surface of the Sun. Areas around sunspots often show brighter patches called faculae. These can also occur apart from sunspots, and are best seen near the limb of the Sun.

Sunspots can occur singly or in groups. Each of these active regions varies in number daily, monthly, and annually.

Large sunspots can generate flares—huge outbursts of energy that shoot high-energy, fast-moving particles far into the solar system.

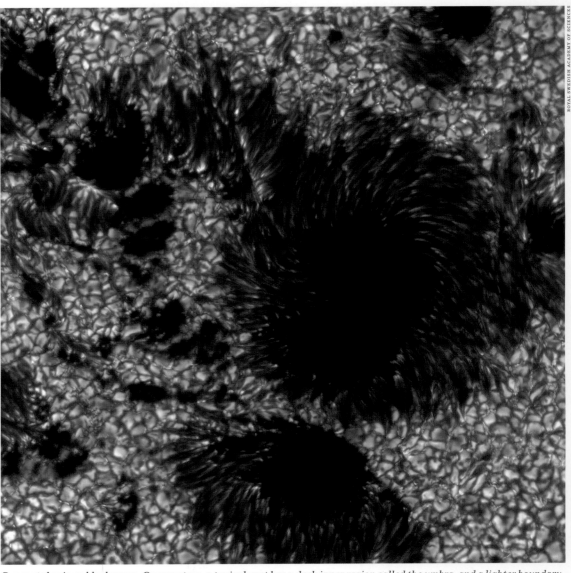

Sunspots begin as black pores. Once mature, a typical spot has a dark inner region called the umbra, and a lighter boundary called the penumbra. Some sunspots grow into very complex regions, such as this one, and changes in their structure are noticeable over a few hours.

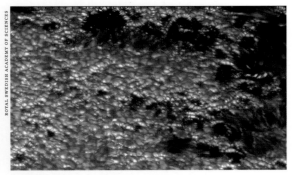

A new telescope operated by the Swedish Academy of Sciences in the Canary Islands takes the most finely detailed ground-based images of the Sun ever recorded. Visible here are 600-mile-wide roiling, bubbling granules and bright white "faculae" on the surface of the Sun.

Sometimes they reach Earth, and disrupt radio communications and trigger electrical outages. They also produce beautiful auroras (northern and southern lights).

SUN FACTS

The diameter of the Sun is a staggering 109 times that of planet Earth. Yet studies of the galaxy of stars show the Sun to be a relatively ordinary yellow dwarf star compared to many others. There are stars in our galaxy 100 times as massive as our Sun.

The enormous energy of our Sun reaches us in the form of light and heat. It takes eight minutes for light to travel the nearly 93 million miles from the center of the solar system to Earth. When it reaches us, its energy forms the basis for all life on our planet.

The Sun's outer atmosphere is called the corona. Its pearly white, gossamer glow around a totally eclipsed Sun is one of nature's grandest sights. The temperature here rises to an average of 2 million degrees Fahrenheit. The power to heat the corona comes from the Sun's intense magnetic field, though how this occurs is a mystery.

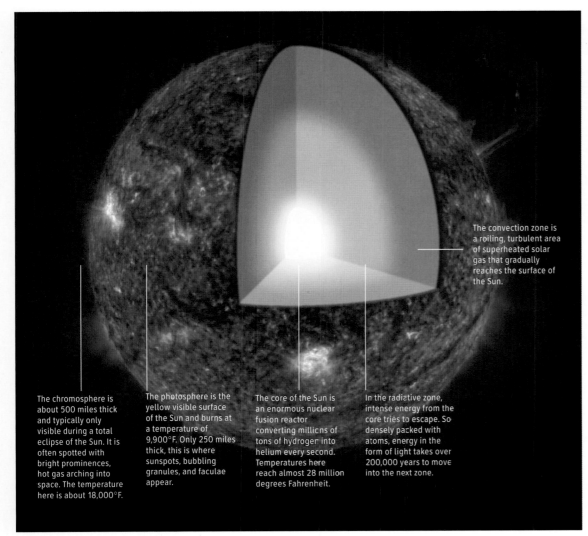

SUN DATA

Diameter	865,000 miles
Mass [1]	333,400
Average Density [2]	1.4 g/cm³
Gravity [1]	27.9
Escape Velocity	384 miles per second
Rotation Period	25.4 days
Inclination to ecliptic	7° 15'
Surface Temperature	9,900°F
Luminosity	3.83×10^{26} joules/second

[1] (Earth = 1)
[2] (Water = 1)

The convection zone is a roiling, turbulent area of superheated solar gas that gradually reaches the surface of the Sun.

The chromosphere is about 500 miles thick and typically only visible during a total eclipse of the Sun. It is often spotted with bright prominences, hot gas arching into space. The temperature here is about 18,000°F.

The photosphere is the yellow visible surface of the Sun and burns at a temperature of 9,900°F. Only 250 miles thick, this is where sunspots, bubbling granules, and faculae appear.

The core of the Sun is an enormous nuclear fusion reactor converting millions of tons of hydrogen into helium every second. Temperatures here reach almost 28 million degrees Fahrenheit.

In the radiative zone, intense energy from the core tries to escape. So densely packed with atoms, energy in the form of light takes over 200,000 years to move into the next zone.

This illustration shows the intensity of our central star, radiating its nuclear fusion energy across the solar system and out into the galaxy. The arching solar prominence in the upper right of this illustration reaches out over twenty times the diameter of the Earth.

This composite image of a solar eclipse shows the phases leading up to and following totality. A total eclipse is the only way to observe the corona, the outer atmosphere, of the Sun from Earth. Other features, such as prominences, and Baily's Beads—bright areas around the edge of the disk— may also be observed during totality.

LIFE OF THE SUN

Our Sun is about 5 billion years old—it's roughly middle-aged. In about 5 billion years from now the Sun will begin to run out of fuel and expand into what is known as a red giant. The outer edge of the giant will stretch beyond Earth's orbit to Mars, swallowing the inner planets. Eventually the star will eject its expanded atmosphere, forming a planetary nebula, leaving behind a diminished white dwarf star.

SOLAR ECLIPSES

A total eclipse of the Sun is one of the most spectacular of all natural phenomena. Sunlight is, for a few brief minutes, completely cut off from view.

Eclipses of the Sun occur at new Moon, when the Earth, Moon, and Sun are exactly in line. This does not happen every month because of the tilt of the Moon's orbit. At least two eclipses of the Sun occur every year, and in some years as many as five.

When the alignment is perfect, either an annular or a total eclipse occurs. The type of eclipse depends on the Moon's distance from Earth. The Moon's orbit is elliptical, which carries the Moon nearer or farther from the Earth at different times. If the Moon is near apogee when an eclipse occurs, the Moon's disk will be too small to cover the Sun entirely. At mid-eclipse, a bright ring of light, or annulus, will remain.

CAUTION: VIEWING THE TOTAL PHASE OF AN ECLIPSE IS SAFE WITHOUT EYE PROTECTION, BUT TAKE GREAT CARE NEAR THE END OF THE ECLIPSE AND DURING THE ENTIRE PARTIAL PHASES. WHEN EVEN A SLIVER OF THE SUN'S SURFACE IS VISIBLE, YOUR EYESIGHT IS IN DANGER AND PROTECTIVE FILTERS ARE A NECESSITY.

FRED ESPENAK/WWW.MRECLIPSE.COM

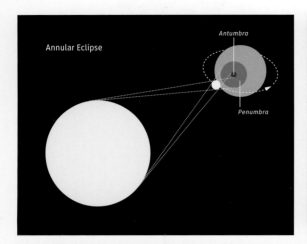

Annular Eclipse

Antumbra

Penumbra

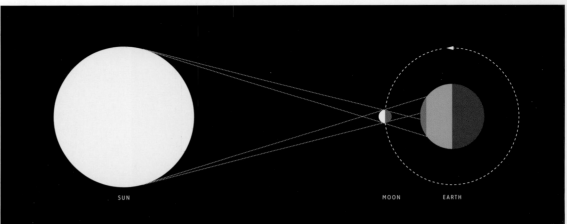

SUN   MOON   EARTH

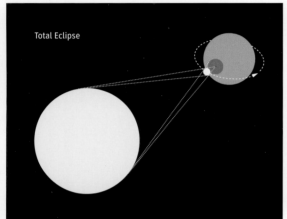

Total Eclipse

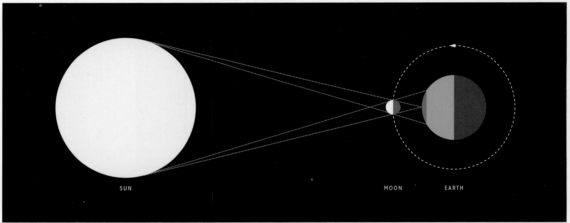

SUN   MOON   EARTH

Two types of solar eclipses, annular and total, take place when the Moon passes in front of the Sun. Unfortunately, an annular eclipse visible from North America will not take place until May 20, 2012. On August 21, 2017, a total eclipse of the Sun will be viewable across the United States. Charts of eclipse visibility across the Earth are available online from NASA and the US Naval Observatory.

The longest an annular eclipse can last is twelve-and-a-half minutes.

The rarest form of eclipse is a hybrid—a combination of an annular and total eclipse. Only six of this type of eclipse occur per century. Part of the track is total, but at some point the curvature of the Earth is enough for the shadow of the Moon to end just above the surface, leaving a ring of light around the Sun, as in an annular eclipse. These hybrid eclipses occur when the Moon and Sun are exactly the same apparent size. The last one to occur was in April 2005. The next one is in 2013.

SOLAR ECLIPSES FROM LATE 2007–2012

YEAR	DATE	TYPE	DURATION	REGION OF VISIBILITY
2007	Sep 11	Partial	–	Antarctica, S. America
2008	Feb 7	Annular	–	Antarctica
2008	Aug 1	Total	2m 27s	Canada, N. Greenland, Russia, Kazakstan, Mongolia, China
2009	Jan 26	Annular	7m 53s	S. Indian Ocean, Indonesia
2009	Jul 22	Total	6m 38s	India, Nepal, China, Pacific Ocean
2010	Jan 15	Annular	11m 7s	Chad, Cameroon, Dem. Rep. of the Congo, Uganda, Kenya, Somalia, India, Sri Lanka, Bangladesh, Myanmar, China
2010	Jul 11	Total	5m 20s	S. Pacific, Chile, Argentina
2012	May 20	Annular	5m 47s	China, Japan, N. Pacific, SW U.S.A.
2012	Nov 13	Total	4m 02s	N. Australia, South Pacific Ocean

Mercury

OBSERVING MERCURY

Mercury speeds around the Sun in 88 days and is viewed alternately to the east and west of the Sun as seen from Earth. When Mercury lies east of the Sun, it appears in the evening sky, and when west, it's visible in the morning sky.

Mercury is the innermost planet in our solar system and never strays far from the Sun's tight gravitational leash. At best, Mercury can reach as far as 27° away from our central star, though typically this value is closer to 20°. Even when it is well placed for observation, the period of visibility of Mercury lasts only about three weeks. It appears near the horizon at dawn or dusk, always in twilight.

The best period for viewing Mercury is around the time of maximum elongation and when the ecliptic sits at a high angle to the horizon. This places Mercury higher in the sky

Four planets lie along the ecliptic in this twilight photograph—Mercury, Venus, Mars, and Saturn. Mars and Saturn form a triangle with the star Aldebaran in Taurus. On this occasion, Mercury was 16° east of the Sun. The Pleiades (M45) lies to the upper right of Venus and Orion appears to the left.

and results in later setting times to get a view of Mercury in a darker sky.

For the northern hemisphere, the steep ecliptic occurs in March evenings and September mornings. Unfortunately, Mercury is near perihelion at these times, resulting in smaller elongations of only 18°–20°. When Mercury is at aphelion, producing larger

Left bottom: Mercury's orbit is tilted 7° to Earth's orbit—the ecliptic. The tilt is exaggerated here to show that Mercury rarely crosses directly in front of the Sun as seen from Earth. Left top: The elliptical orbit of Mercury carries the planet through varying distances from the Sun. Right top: An example in 2007 showing the changing location of Mercury relative to the Earth. Dotted lines show the line of sight from Earth. Right bottom: Earth and Mercury's conjunctions and elongation points; orbits are shown as circular for simplicity.

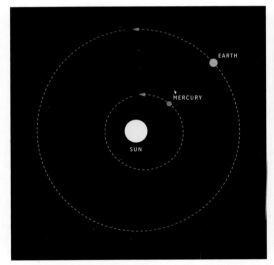

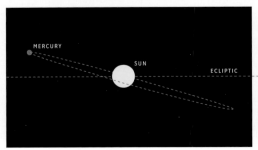

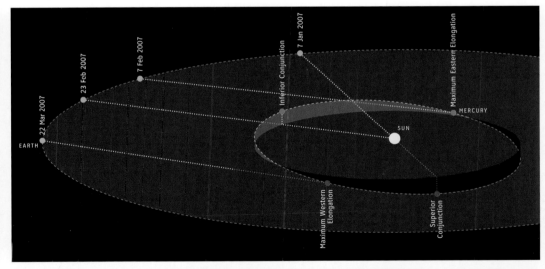

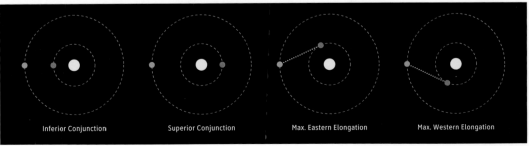

This sequence of telescopic images shows a transit of Mercury (east to west) as seen from Earth. The enormous orange limb of the Sun provides the background for the tiny black disk of the planet.

elongation angles from the Sun, Mercury sits south of the celestial equator, a factor favoring southern hemisphere observers, but poor for those in the northern hemisphere.

While Mercury travels around the Sun it goes through phases, rather like the Moon. You need a telescope to follow them. When Mercury appears in the evening sky, it is traveling from the far side of the Sun to a point between the Sun and Earth. Its swing to the east of the Sun takes Mercury through phases from full to a thin crescent. During this period, the apparent size of Mercury changes, growing larger as it moves nearer to Earth.

The reverse happens during a morning apparition. After Mercury has passed between the Earth and Sun, it moves to the west, and grows from a thin crescent to a full disk.

Mercury is disappointing when seen through a telescope. Details of the tiny planet are not visible. However, developments in digital imaging from Earth-based telescopes have begun to produce startling results. This marvelous digital photograph by Ron Dantowitz is the best Earth-based photograph of Mercury yet obtained. It is shown here shortly before greatest western elongation.

USE CAUTION WHEN LOOKING FOR MERCURY IN DAYLIGHT. THE PLANET IS SO CLOSE TO THE SUN THAT THERE IS A RISK OF ACCIDENTALLY LOOKING STRAIGHT AT THE SUN WITH BINOCULARS OR TELESCOPE. BLINDNESS WILL RESULT.

These changes directly affect the brightness of Mercury. It is brightest near a gibbous phase, and dims as it progresses to a crescent. As Mercury becomes closer to the Earth, this modifies the drop in brightness slightly, but the phases have the most impact on Mercury's brightness.

During an evening elongation, Mercury can be viewed about 30 minutes after sunset. Initially the phase of Mercury is nearly full, and shrinks during the short period of visibility to a half phase, and then to a crescent. Fading quickly, Mercury becomes lower in the sky relative to the Sun each day, and becomes lost in the evening twilight. Mercury then passes through inferior conjunction and into the morning sky.

TRANSITS OF MERCURY

If Mercury's orbit were precisely in the plane of the ecliptic, every time Mercury passed between the Earth and Sun, which occurs every 116 days, a transit of Mercury would occur. There would be a transit every inferior conjunction. However, the severe inclination of Mercury's orbit to the plane of the ecliptic usually causes Mercury to miss the Sun, passing north or south of the solar disk.

The points of Mercury's orbit that cross the ecliptic are called the nodes. The nodes are in line with the Sun as seen from Earth on or near May 8 and November 10. If Mercury reaches inferior conjunction on those dates, a transit will occur. Transits of Mercury occur at regular intervals of 13 or 33 years, plus a combination of these two at 46 years. After such periods, the Earth and Mercury have returned to almost the same points in their orbits and the pattern repeats. The next transits occur on May 9, 2016 and November 11, 2019.

Mariner 10 transmitted data for this photomosaic image of Mercury in the 1970s. Missing data is shown blank. The Messenger spacecraft, launched in 2004, will fill in the details and much more between 2008–2011.

MERCURY DATA

Diameter	3,031 miles
Distance from Sun	Max: 0.467 a.u. 43.8 mil. mi. Min: 0.308 a.u. 28.6 mil. mi.
Rotation Period	58.65 days
Sidereal Period	87.97 days
Mean Synodic Period	115.88 days
Orbital Inclination	7° 0'18"
Inclination of Axis	0°
Apparent Diameter	Max: 12.3" Min: 4.5"
Albedo	0.11
Mass [1]	0.055
Density [2]	5.44
Surface Gravity [1]	0.38
Escape Velocity	2.6 miles per second

[1] (Earth = 1)

[2] (Water = 1)

PLANETARY FACTS

Mercury is the smallest of the four inner rocky planets of our solar system. Aside from Pluto, it is the least explored planetary surface. The entire globe has still not been completely mapped by spacecraft.

Mercury's enigmatic world undergoes wild variations in surface temperature, varying from a frigidly cold −300°F on the dark side to a scorchingly hot 765°F on the sunward hemisphere.

Part of the reason for the lack of missions to Mercury is the difficulty of getting there. The seemingly simple hop to an inner planet is complicated by its high orbital speed averaging 30 miles per second. Matching this speed is a complicated maneuver for a spacecraft that is limited by the amount of fuel it can carry.

Early observations of Mercury revealed slight variations in brightness, indicating some surface features. The tiny disk, however, refused to yield its secrets. Our turbulent atmosphere constantly buffets telescopic views of Mercury, and high contrast imaging is impossible given the proximity of the planet to the Sun. It was not until the early 1970s that Mercury's hidden surface began to be unveiled in all its pitted glory.

The only spacecraft ever to visit Mercury in the 20th century was Mariner 10. In one of the early successes of interplanetary exploration, and despite several serious setbacks during the mission, from 1974 to 1975 the spacecraft sent back dozens of pictures of the surface. These images remain our only record of Mercury so far. The unseen side of Mercury, more than half the planet, hides unknown secrets.

SURFACE

Mariner 10 revealed a surface that appeared rather like our own Moon, covered in impact craters. However, unlike the Moon, the heavily cratered upland regions are covered with smooth plains. Many craters exhibit bright ray structures like those seen on the lunar surface.

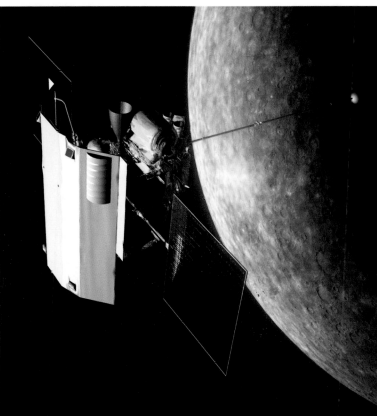

*Launched on August 3, 2004, Messenger (**ME**rcury, **S**urface, **S**pace **EN**vironment, **GE**ochemistry, and **R**anging) will send back unprecedented information about our innermost planet. After three flybys, the Messenger spacecraft will take up orbit around Mercury on March 18, 2011.*

The largest feature on the surface appears to be a giant impact basin. The Caloris Basin spans nearly one quarter of the diameter of Mercury, covering over 800 miles. The region directly opposite the Caloris basin, in the other hemisphere of Mercury, reveals a hilly region that may have been formed by the focus of planetary shock waves wrapping around the planet from the Caloris impact.

Mariner 10 photographed half of the Caloris basin. The remainder was out of view from its brief flyby mission. Once the Messenger spacecraft arrives in 2011, the multi-ringed basin will be the target of a detailed photo-reconnaissance.

GRAVITY

Mercury's small size but large mass generates stronger gravity than would be expected for a planet this size. Mercury is 30 percent smaller than Mars, yet has a similar gravitational pull. Mercury is made of heavier material than Mars. In fact, careful measurements show that Mercury probably has a core of iron that makes up 70 percent of the planet's mass, twice as much as any other object in the solar system.

MAGNETIC FIELD

Mercury has a magnetic field about 1 percent of the strength of Earth's magnetic field and is tilted 11° from its rotation axis. The origin of the magnetic field, usually ascribed to motion of molten iron, is not well understood in the case of Mercury. Future data from the Messenger spacecraft may reveal significant facts about the inner workings of the planet.

A DAY ON MERCURY

The combination of the fast orbital motion and varying distance from the Sun makes a day on Mercury peculiar when compared to our experience on Earth. During every two orbits of the Sun, Mercury rotates three times on its axis. If you could view the Sun rising when Mercury is at aphelion, the Sun appears twice as big as it does on Earth.

The Sun reaches its noon position 44 Earth days later, a very long morning by our standards. Mercury also reaches perihelion around the same time, and the Sun appears three times larger than it does on Earth. It performs an odd loop, since the orbital speed is much faster at perihelion, causing the Sun to wander "backwards" briefly in the sky. Also, the temperature rises by more than 1,000°F from dawn. Forty-four days later the Sun sets and Mercury has returned to aphelion. Eighty-eight days of night follow, when Mercury travels one more entire orbit of the Sun, and a massive drop in temperature occurs. Just before the next dawn, the frigid cold of −300°F returns.

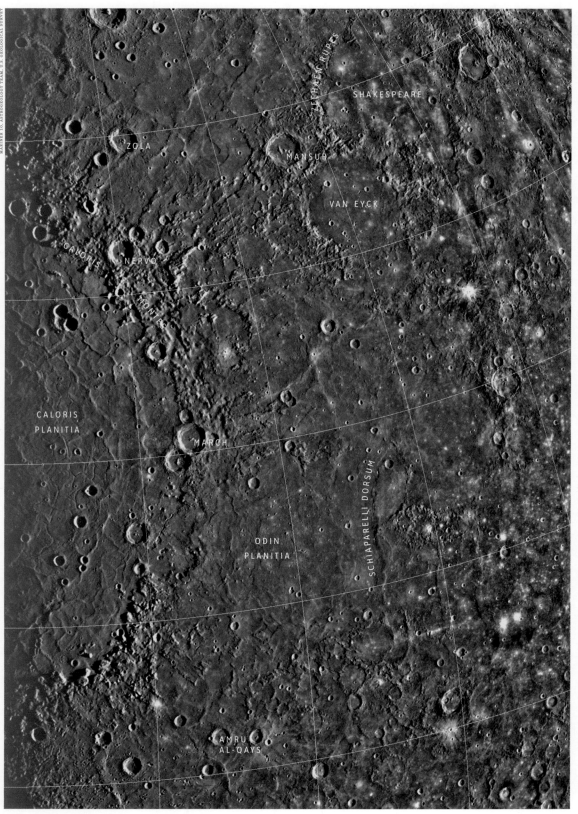

INFERIOR CONJUNCTION		SUPERIOR CONJUNCTION	
YEAR	DATE	YEAR	DATE
2007	Jun 28	2007	Aug 15
2007	Oct 23	2007	Dec 17
2008	Feb 6	2008	Apr 16
2008	Jun 7	2008	Jul 29
2008	Oct 6	2008	Nov 25
2009	Jan 20	2009	Mar 31
2009	May 18	2009	Jul 14
2009	Sep 20	2009	Nov 5
2010	Jan 4	2010	Mar 14
2010	Apr 28	2010	Jun 28
2010	Sep 3	2010	Oct 17
2010	Dec 20	2011	Feb 25
2011	Apr 9	2011	Jun 12
2011	Aug 17	2011	Sep 28
2011	Dec 4	2012	Feb 7
2012	Mar 21	2012	May 27
2012	Jul 28	2012	Sep 10
2012	Nov 17		

WESTERN ELONGATION (MORNING APPEAR.)			EASTERN ELONGATION (EVENING APPEAR.)		
YEAR	DATE	DEG.	YEAR	DATE	DEG.
2007	Jul 20	20°	2007	Jun 2	23°
2007	Nov 8	19°	2007	Sep 29	26°
2008	Mar 3	27°	2008	Jan 22	19°
2008	Jul 1	22°	2008	May 14	22°
2008	Oct 22	18°	2008	Sep 11	27°
2009	Feb 13	26°	2009	Jan 4	19°
2009	Jul 13	23°	2009	Apr 26	20°
2009	Oct 6	18°	2009	Aug 24	27°
2010	Jan 27	25°	2009	Dec 18	20°
2010	May 26	25°	2010	Apr 8	19°
2010	Sep 19	18°	2010	Aug 7	27°
2011	Jan 9	23°	2010	Dec 1	21°
2011	May 7	27°	2011	Mar 23	19°
2011	Sep 3	18°	2011	Jul 20	27°
2011	Dec 23	22°	2011	Nov 14	23°
2012	Apr 18	28°	2012	Mar 5	18°
2012	Aug 16	19°	2012	Jul 1	26°
2012	Dec 4	21°	2012	Oct 26	24°

The 800-mile-wide Caloris basin is partly shown at left in this photomosaic from Mariner 10. Scientists will have to wait for the arrival of Messenger to complete the view. Striking among Mercury's features are huge scarps, in some cases hundreds of miles long, snaking across the battered surface of the planet. The leading theory of their origin suggests that the planet underwent cooling that caused it to shrink a few miles in diameter, causing huge faults leading to the formation of long cliffs.

Venus

OBSERVING VENUS

Venus is the brightest object in the sky after the Sun and Moon. It can reach magnitude −4.5, 17 times brighter than Sirius, the brightest star in the sky. Because Venus orbits relatively close to the Sun, it never strays far in angular distance from our local star. Its orbit carries it to the west and east of the Sun, causing Venus to appear alternately in the morning and evening sky. These brilliant appearances have given Venus the two nicknames, "Evening Star" and "Morning Star," although Venus is, of course, not a star at all. The farthest Venus treks is about 47° away from the Sun. At this angular distance, Venus can set more than three hours after the Sun and shine brilliantly in a dark sky.

As Venus orbits the Sun, it progresses though a series of phases just like our own Moon. Superior conjunction occurs when Venus lies on the opposite side of the Sun to the Earth. For a period, we see the fully illuminated, dayside face of Venus.

Following superior conjunction, the angular distance of Venus from the Sun increases and it becomes visible in the western sky after sunset. At first, when viewed through a telescope, the disk is fairly small, but each day the disk grows in size as the phase diminishes. When it reaches 50 percent illumination, the planet spans double the apparent size when it was full. (See illustration upper right.) It has also reached greatest elongation east of the Sun and is visible high in the western sky, setting at least three hours after the Sun.

As Venus continues around its orbit, the phase shrinks to a thin crescent before passing between the Earth and Sun at inferior conjunction. Venus passes into the morning sky and performs the reverse series of phases and a shrinking disk appears through a telescope. The average period between two successive superior conjunctions is 584 days.

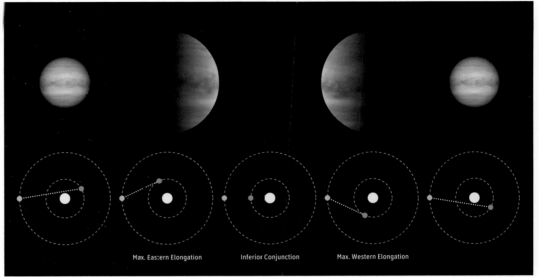

Max. Eastern Elongation   Inferior Conjunction   Max. Western Elongation

MARTIN RATCLIFFE

Venus passes through phases just like the Moon. The top row shows an enhanced appearance of Venus, and below each picture is a corresponding diagram showing the relevant geometry of Earth, Sun, and Venus. The dark side of Venus faces Earth at inferior conjunction and is invisible.

Venus shines brightly in Gemini on March 22, 2004, a month when the ecliptic is angled high relative to the horizon. The Pleiades is near the top, and Mars is to its left. The crescent Moon lies just above the house, and Mercury is nestled in the twilight glow.

Favorable elongations of Venus occur when the ecliptic is inclined steeply to the horizon. On these occasions, such as in springtime for evening views, as the planet's elongation increases, the period of time that Venus sets after the Sun increases significantly.

During fall evenings, however, the ecliptic has a shallow angle with the horizon. As its elongation increases, Venus simply sets farther south along the horizon, with little change to the time it sets after the Sun.

In the morning sky the timing of favorable elongations of Venus is reversed. The ecliptic has a shallow angle to the horizon in spring and a steep angle in the fall. During the favorable periods, Venus is crossing the constellations of the northern ecliptic, including Aries, Taurus, Gemini, and Cancer.

Venus is bright enough to be spotted with the naked eye in daylight near one of its greatest elongations. The best way to do this is during an early morning when Venus is visible before sunrise. Locate Venus in twilight and pick a static reference point, such as a telephone pole or prominent tree, and then keep watch on its position until after sunrise.

PLANETARY FACTS

Venus is Earth's fiery twin. In fact, the Venusian atmosphere causes the surface temperature to be hotter than Mercury, even though it is farther from the Sun. The second planet from the Sun, Venus is only 400 miles smaller in diameter than our home planet and has a similar density, but that's where the similarity ends. Venus has a crushingly thick atmosphere of carbon dioxide, deadly rain of sulfuric acid, and a searing surface temperature of 900°F. It's hot enough there to melt lead and zinc.

The high temperature on Venus is caused by a runaway greenhouse effect, where light from the Sun penetrates to the surface, but the blanket of carbon dioxide in the air is thick enough to block the radiating heat.

The brilliance of Venus in the morning and evening skies is due to the atmosphere reflecting 76 percent of sunlight back into space. Telescopic views of the planet reveal phases, yet no detail is visible on the surface. The thick atmosphere hides any direct views.

ROTATION

Venus has a peculiar rotation and is unlike any other planet. It rotates backwards in a period longer than it takes to orbit the Sun. Consequently, its day is longer than its year. It rotates from east to west, whereas all other planets rotate from west to east. An observer on the surface would see the Sun rise in the west and set in the east. The rotation period is 243 days, 18 days longer than its year. The combination of the 243-day rotation period and 225-day orbital period is a 117-day solar day, the period from one sunrise to the next.

Each time Venus returns to the same location in our sky, every 584 days, it has gone through only five solar days. This results in observations from Earth seeing the same face of Venus each time it appears closest to Earth.

There is also an orbital resonance. Every eight Earth years is the same as five synodic periods (584 days). This results in Venus repeating its five traces across the sky every eight years. This synchronicity was known to the Mayan civilization. The 260-day length of the morning or evening visibility period was used as the basis for the Mayan calendar.

This image from the Hubble Space Telescope in ultraviolet light shows Venus completely covered with clouds. A Y-shaped cloud feature is visible near the equator indicating atmospheric activity not seen from Earth-based instruments.

VENUS DATA

Diameter	7,521 miles
Distance from Sun	Max: 0.729 a.u. 67.73 mil. mi. Min: 0.718 a.u. 66.74 mil. mi.
Rotation Period	243 days (retrograde)
Sidereal Period	224.7 days
Mean Synodic Period	583.92 days
Orbital Inclination	3° 23'24"
Inclination of Axis	177.4°
Apparent Diameter	Max: 63.1" Min: 9.6"
Albedo	0.65
Mass [1]	0.82
Density [2]	5.24
Surface Gravity [1]	0.88
Escape Velocity	6.4 miles per second

[1] (Earth = 1)
[2] (Water = 1)

EXPLORATION OF VENUS

Landing any spacecraft on the surface of Venus is a most serious and challenging engineering task. Since lead melts on the surface, and corrosive rain dissolves metal, a spacecraft will not last very long. The Soviet Venera spacecraft achieved eight successful landings (Veneras 7–14) between August 1970 and November 1981. These are the only missions that have returned images from the surface of the planet.

This amazing image of the surface of Venus, taken by Venera 10 on October 27, 1975, is one of a series of the first views ever broadcast from another planet. Venera 10 lasted 65 minutes on the surface before succumbing to the harsh environment. Its sister craft, Venera 9, landed five days earlier and 150 miles away, and revealed a similar scene of sharp edged rocks.

ВЕНЕРА-9   22.10.1975   ОБРАБОТКА ИППИ АН СССР   28.2.1976

This composite image is made from multiple radar passes over the surface of Venus taken by the Magellan mission. The image is color-coded to represent elevation, with blue showing the lowest elevations, then through green, orange, red, and the very highest regions shown in white.

Radar images from orbit around Venus have provided the most detailed global look at the planet. The most recent, and most successful, was the Magellan mission. Magellan became a satellite of Venus (the planet has no natural moons) for four years, from 1990 to 1994. Each orbit provided a narrow swath of radar imagery that was eventually stitched together into a detailed global view. Magellan approached as close as 182 miles and was able to resolve detail as small as 400 feet across. By the time Magellan made a fiery descent into the Venusian atmosphere, gaining data about the atmosphere as it went, 98 percent of the planet had been mapped.

   The most remarkable images from this mission were the three-dimensional views that could be reconstructed from the data. These gave unprecedented and unique views of the Venusian surface. Due to the high surface temperature,

Above right: A portion of western Eistla Regio is shown in this three dimensional, computer-generated view of the surface of Venus. The view is of 1.8-mile high Gula Mons, the volcano on the right horizon. Radar and height data from the Magellan spacecraft were used to generate this view. Bottom right: Pancake domes are an unusual feature on Venus. These circular, steep-sided volcanic structures are about 15 miles across and 2,500 feet high. Their formation is due to viscous lava seeping up through the planet's crust.

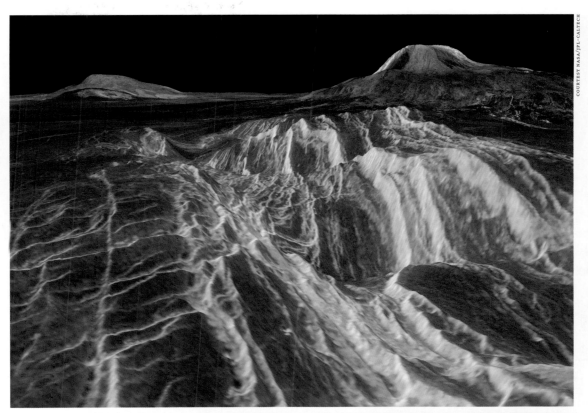

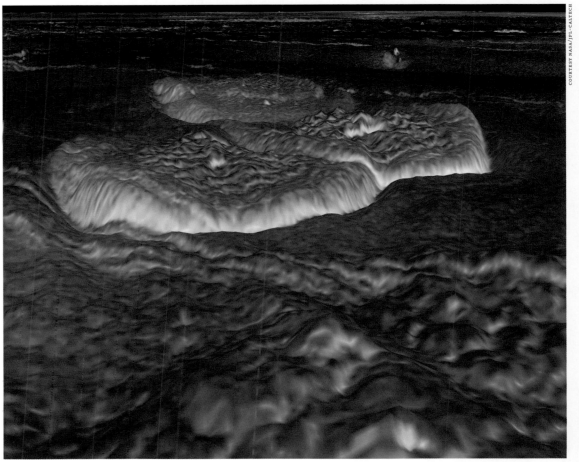

rock on the surface is fluid. Mountains will eventually flatten out unless re-built by continuing volcanic activity.

One unique surface feature on Venus is the Coronae, concentric rings of ridges and fractures with central mounds or low depressions in the center. Most are between one and two hundred miles across, although one reaches ten times this size. No features quite like these are found on other planets. They are thought to have formed from buoyant blobs of rock slowly ascending and cooling and deforming the surface.

Relatively few impact craters are found on Venus. This is not surprising considering the thick atmosphere, which is capable of wearing down any incoming lump of rock to dust. There are a few large impact features, yet all are remarkably well preserved.

TRANSITS OF VENUS

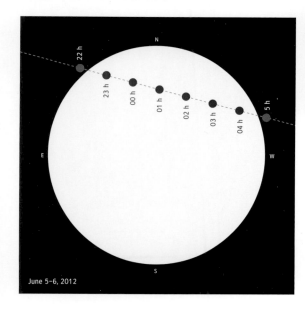

June 5–6, 2012

Transits of Venus are very rare. There are on average two transits of Venus every 125 years. The last one to occur was on June 8, 2004. The next one will be on June 5–6, 2012. After that, there will be a long wait until the next event, which will occur on December 11, 2117.

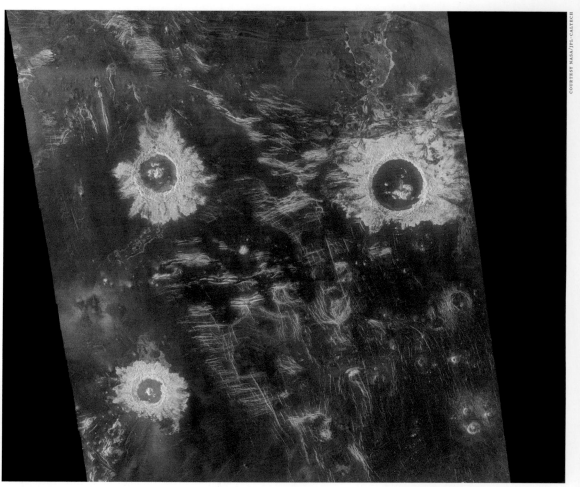

COURTESY NASA/JPL-CALTECH

Three large meteorite impact craters with diameters that range from 23 to 31 miles, are seen in this image of the Lavinia region of Venus. The Magellan radar image covers an area 342 miles wide by about 311 miles long. The craters show many features typical of meteorite impact craters, including rough (bright) material around the rim, terraced inner walls and central peaks. Considering the harsh Venusian weather, these craters are unusually fresh looking, and indicate that they are relatively new.

VISIBILITY CHART

YEAR	EVENING SKY	MORNING SKY
2007	Jan (SSW)–Jul (W)	Late Aug (E)–Dec (SE)
2008	Aug (W)–Dec (SW)	Jan (SE)–Apr (E)
2009	Jan (SW)–Mar (W)	Ap (E)–Nov (ESE)
2010	Feb (W)–Sep (WSW)	Nov (ESE)–Dec (SE)
2011	Jan (SE)–Jul (ENE)	Sep (W)–Dec (SW)
2012	Jan (SW)–May (WNW)	Jun (ENE)–Dec (SE)

INFERIOR CONJUNCTION		SUPERIOR CONJUNCTION		WESTERN ELONGATION			EASTERN ELONGATION		
YEAR	DATE	YEAR	DATE	YEAR	DATE	DEG.	YEAR	DATE	DEG.
2007	Mar 18	2008	Jun 9	2007	Oct 28	46°	2007	Jun 9	45°
2009	Mar 27	2010	Jan 11	2009	Jun 5	46°	2009	Jan 14	47°
2010	Oct 29	2011	Aug 16	2011	Jan 8	47°	2010	Aug 20	46°
2012	Jun 5			2012	Aug 15	46°	2012	Mar 27	46°

Earth

EARTH IN MOTION

Though we don't have much perception of it, the Earth is constantly in motion. Our planet is both rotating on its axis and speeding in orbit around the Sun. Because of the constant motion of the Earth, we observe the universe from a vantage point of relative motion. The Moon, planets, Sun, and the constellations appear to rotate, too, rising and setting in the same direcxtion through the years from east to west. Understanding Earth's motion and

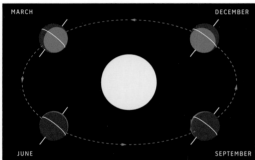

The Earth's axis is tilted by 23.5° to its orbit around the Sun. In June the North Pole is tilted towards the Sun, giving the northern hemisphere summer and the southern hemisphere winter. In December the reverse is true. In March and September Earth experiences equal day and night.

The Earth's tilted axis wobbles like a spinning top, called precession, and it takes 26,000 years for each full wobble. Currently, the Earth's northern axis points towards the star Polaris, but over four thousand years ago it pointed towards Thuban, a star in Draco, the Dragon.

observing the changes in our skies through the years is the essence of astronomy.

The Earth rotates in a period of 23 hours 56 minutes 4.1 seconds. This measurement is determined by watching how long it takes a star to return to the same point in the sky each night. Many of tne world's oldest observatories have fixed instruments pointing along a north-south direction in the sky with the sole purpose of timing the movement of stars from one day to the next.

The Earth completely orbits the Sun in 365.25 days, so each day we move about 1° in orbit. This places the Sun 1° farther east relative to the background stars. Consequently, while the stars return to the same location as seen from Earth in 23 hours 56 minutes, the Earth has to rotate an additional degree for the Sun to do the same, since it lies farther east relative to the stars.

Dividing 24 hours by 360° (the number of degrees in one full circle), we find that the earth turns 1° in four minutes. Adding four minutes to our rotation period gives us the period defined as the length of the day, 24 hours. But what about the four minute difference? Because our system of time runs on a 24-hour clock, and the Earth's rotation is four minutes shorter than this period, the stars rise four minutes earlier every night.

The daily four-minute change amounts to stars rising a full two hours earlier over a period of a month. Consequently we see a seasonal parade of constellations from east to west. Each group rises earlier each week, and each season we see different constellations in the sky. It's a direct result of Earth's orbital motion around the Sun.

PLANETARY FACTS

The Earth is the third planet from the Sun, and is unique within the solar system because of the presence of oxygen in its atmosphere. Oxygen is a highly reactive gas, quickly

combining with other elements such as iron to form rust. Oxygen must also be constantly replenished in our atmosphere through photosynthesis. Sunlight provides the energy for the process of plants taking in carbon dioxide and releasing oxygen. Without this critical cycle, life on our planet as we know it would not be possible.

Oxygen makes up 21 percent of Earth's atmosphere and nitrogen makes up 77 percent. Argon, water vapor, and carbon dioxide make up the remainder. Only one other object in the solar system has a nitrogen atmosphere, Titan, the largest moon of Saturn. With a surface temperature of −289°F, it is considered too cold for the development of life.

The surface of the Earth is one of the most geologically active in the solar system. Oceans cover 60 percent of the surface and land masses make up the other 40 percent. Volcanoes and earthquake zones are sites of frequent activity. Many of these active zones lie along the edges of the major land masses.

Rocks on Earth have been found to have a wide range of ages. The oldest ever found are 4.2 billion years old. Consequently, the Earth must be at least this age. The youngest rocks, near the oceanic ridges, are 200 million years old. Meteorites and Moon rocks are slightly older—between 4.3 and 4.5 billion years. These rocks from space have been flying around the Sun since the formation of the solar system, so they should be slightly older than the Earth.

The surface of the Earth has seams in places where plates of its crust fit together. Earthquakes are shocks created when the crust of the Earth moves suddenly, relieving pressure at the junction of two adjacent plates. The ground vibrates and rolls as the shock waves travel through the crust. Most earthquakes are concentrated around regions of mountain chains.

Volcanoes are scattered across the Earth's surface. Some are dormant or extinct, but a number are very active. The islands of Hawaii

THE TORINO SCALE

The Torino scale shows the relative effects of different sized impacts and how they would affect life on Earth.

WHITE ZONE: EVENTS HAVING NO LIKELY CONSEQUENCES

0	The likelihood of a collision is zero, or well below the chance that a random object of the same size will strike the Earth within the next few decades. This designation also applies to any small object that, in the event of a collision, is unlikely to reach the Earth's surface intact.

GREEN ZONE: EVENTS MERITING CAREFUL MONITORING

1	The chance of collision is extremely unlikely, about the same as a random object of the same size striking the Earth within the next few decades.

YELLOW ZONE: EVENTS MERITING CONCERN

2	A somewhat close, but not unusual encounter. Collision is very unlikely.
3	A close encounter, with 1 percent or greater chance of a collision capable of causing localized destruction.
4	A close encounter, with 1 percent or greater chance of a collision capable of causing regional devastation.

ORANGE ZONE: THREATENING EVENTS

5	A close encounter, with a significant threat of a collision capable of causing regional devastation.
6	A close encounter, with a significant threat of a collision capable of causing a global catastrophe.
7	A close encounter, with an extremely significant threat of a collision capable of causing a global catastrophe.

RED ZONE: CERTAIN COLLISIONS

8	A collision capable of causing localized destruction. Such events occur somewhere on Earth between once per 50 years and once per 1,000 years.
9	A collision capable of causing regional devastation. Such events occur between once per 1,000 years and once per 100,000 years.
10	A collision capable of causing a global climatic catastrophe. Such events occur once per 100,000 years, or less often.

Scale developed by Professor Richard P. Binzel, MIT

Approximately 50,000 years ago, a meteor 150 feet across and weighing roughly 300,000 tons struck the Earth in present-day Arizona. The meteor was traveling at a speed of 40,000 miles per hour when it struck and carved an enormous crater. Today the crater is nearly a mile wide and 570 feet deep.

This detailed view of the two hemispheres of planet Earth (opposite left and right) shows the oceans, solid land, and white clouds in our atmosphere. Earth is unique in the solar system in many ways, but most of all, perhaps, by the presence of an enormous amount of liquid water. It covers over 60 percent of the surface area of Earth.

This extraordinary map of the Earth (opposite bottom) is constructed from hundreds of satellite images taken during clear weather, for an unobstructed view. Note how the eastern side of North and South America fits fairly neatly into the western coasts of Europe and Africa. Geologists have found rock on each side of the Atlantic Ocean showing dramatic similarities. This bolsters other evidence that the continents were once united. Each continent on the Earth is adrift on the molten mantle deep beneath the surface and moves slightly over time. Scientists carefully monitor and record this continental drift from the ground and from space.

are still being formed; as the sea floor moves over a stationary hotspot, each new island is carried to the northwest. The big island of Hawaii is still active and growing. Its main vent, Kilauea, on the lower flanks of Mauna Loa, is continuously pumping lava into the sea and building new land.

EARTH AT RISK

Earth is a tiny planet floating around the solar system. Aside from pollution and overpopulation problems, there are risks to living on one planet alone. Life on the surface is susceptible to sudden change, either by geological forces from within the planet, or by impacts from space. The two chief concerns are threats from supervolcanoes and asteroid impacts.

EARTH FACTS

Diameter	7,926 miles	
Distance from Sun	Max: 1.017 a.u.	94.54 mil. mi.
	Min: 0.983 a.u.	91.38 mil. mi.
Rotation Period	23h 56m 4s	
Orbital Inclination	0° (orbit defines the ecliptic plane)	
Inclination of Axis	23.5°	
Albedo	0.37	
Mass	5.97×10^{24} kg	
Density[1]	5.52	
Surface Gravity[2]	1	
Escape Velocity	6.96 miles per second	
Satellites	1	

[1] (Water = 1)
[2] (Earth = 1)

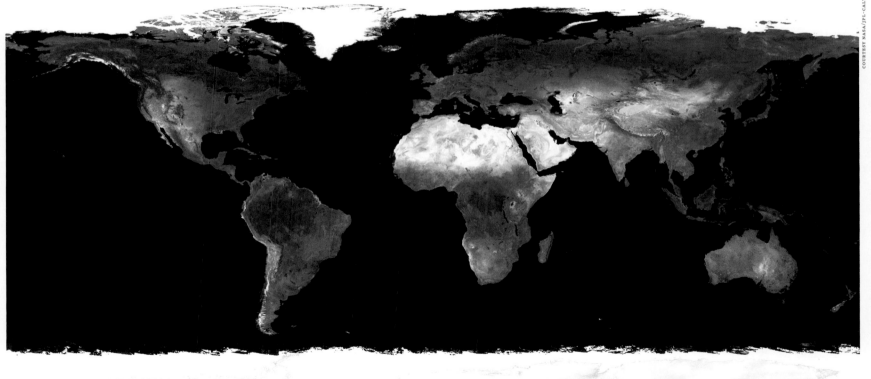

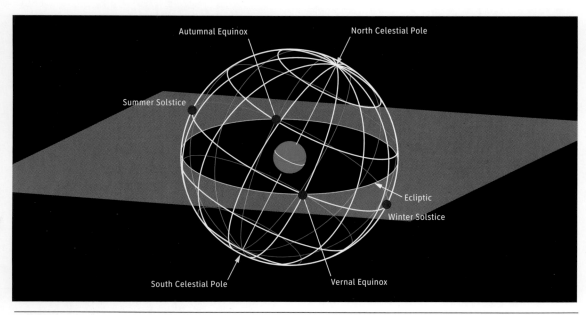

Autumnal Equinox · North Celestial Pole · Summer Solstice · Ecliptic · Winter Solstice · South Celestial Pole · Vernal Equinox

The two points where the ecliptic crosses the celestial equator are called the equinoxes. The Sun, during its annual travel around the ecliptic, crosses these points around March 20 and September 23 each year.

The two points where the ecliptic reaches its highest point north and south of the celestial equator are called the solstices. When the Sun sits at the northernmost point, it is summer in the northern hemisphere. When the Sun reaches the southern extreme, it is winter in the northern hemisphere. The seasons are reversed for the southern hemisphere. The Sun reaches these positions near June 21 and December 21 each year. The exact times are indicated in the table at left.

EARTH EQUINOXES AND SOLSTICES, 2007–2012

Times are given in Universal Time (Greenwich Mean Time). For Eastern Standard Time, subtract five hours. For Central Standard Time, subtract six hours. For Mountain Standard Time, subtract seven hours. For Pacific Standard Time, subtract eight hours. During Daylight Savings Time, subtract one hour less.

	VERNAL EQUINOX	SUMMER SOLSTICE	AUTUMNAL EQUINOX	WINTER SOLSTICE
2007	Mar 21, 00h, 07m	Jun 21, 18h, 06m	Sep 23, 09h, 51m	Dec 22, 06h, 08m
2008	Mar 20, 05h, 48m	Jun 20, 23h, 59m	Sep 22, 15h, 44m	Dec 21, 12h, 04m
2009	Mar 20, 11h, 44m	Jun 21, 05h, 45m	Sep 22, 21h, 18m	Dec 21, 17h, 47m
2010	Mar 29, 17h, 32m	Jun 21, 11h, 28m	Sep 23, 09h, 04m	Dec 21, 23h, 38m
2011	Mar 20, 23h, 21m	Jun 21, 17h, 16m	Sep 23, 09h, 04m	Dec 22, 05h, 30m
2012	Mar 20, 05h, 14m	Jun 20, 23h, 09m	Sep 22, 14h, 49m	Dec 21, 11h, 11m

EARTH PERIHELIONS AND APHELIONS, 2007–2012

The Earth's orbit around the Sun is elliptical, not a perfect circle. Perihelion, Earth's closest point to the Sun occurs in January. Aphelion, Earth's farthest point from the Sun, occurs in July.

2007	Perihelion	Jan 3
	Aphelion	Jul 7
2008	Perihelion	Jan 3
	Aphelion	Jul 4
2009	Perihelion	Jan 4
	Aphelion	Jul 4
2010	Perihelion	Jan 3
	Aphelion	Jul 6
2011	Perihelion	Jan 3
	Aphelion	Jul 4
2012	Perihelion	Jan 5
	Aphelion	Jul 5

The recognition of supervolcanoes is a relatively recent discovery. Beneath the Earth's surface lie huge reservoirs of molten magma that when released create destructive eruptions unlike anything witnessed by humans. Supervolcanoes explode with a force at least one thousand times that of ordinary volcanoes. The last one to erupt was in Toba, Sumatra, 74,000 years ago.

In North America, most of Yellowstone National Park is a huge caldera formed by the last explosion 640,000 years ago. At least three previous eruptions have been identified and date from 640,000 years, 1.2 million years, and 1.8 million years. Given the period of eruptions, every 600,000 years or so, Yellowstone is overdue, on a geological timescale at least. Another eruption could occur in the next ten thousand years; most of North America will be disrupted when it does. It

represents the most significant threat to civilization on the planet.

Today the solar system is a relatively benign place to live, but it is not without risk. The last large impact on Earth was in 1908 when an object entered Earth's atmosphere, exploded, and leveled a huge forest near Tunguska, Siberia.

Each day about 25 tons of dust and grit-sized particles rain down on Earth. Objects about the size of a car strike the Earth once per year. Most objects burn up in the atmosphere before reaching the ground and damage from a meteor striking the Earth is very rare. An asteroid 300 feet across impacts the Earth once per thousand years and would severely affect the local area.

The real danger comes from asteroids larger than half a mile wide. Large impacts that could threaten civilization have occurred in the past, and may occur in the future, though they only occur every few million years.

The Moon

OBSERVING THE MOON

The Moon is the Earth's sole natural satellite and it offers us a bright and lovely subject for observation throughout the year. Through a pair of binoculars or telescope, its carved surface offers amazingly detailed views of giant craters, tall mountains, and vast plains.

The most noticeable feature of the Moon is its different phases. The percentage of the Moon illuminated by the Sun changes each night and after a new Moon, the crescent grows until it reaches full Moon over a two-week period, when it is visible all night.

Following full Moon, the phase begins to diminish back to a crescent. During this period, the Moon rises increasingly later each night after sunset. The cycle from one phase to the next, called a lunation, is 29.53 days, and is so regular that it's useful as a calendar. In fact, the origin of our monthly calendar comes from its near 30-day period.

Various light and dark patches on the Moon are visible with the naked eye. The light areas are the rugged lunar highlands, densely cratered regions with many mountain chains. The darker regions are called mare (plural maria), meaning "sea" in Latin. The maria aren't seas of course, they are level plains of solidified lava. The maria contain relatively few craters, which contrast with surrounding craggy, pitted, and mountainous areas. Because they seemed so relatively featureless, early observers thought they might be oceans, such as the vast seas of Earth.

Many of the Moon's major features come sharply into view through medium-powered

binoculars. With a steady hand or mount, the largest craters and many mountain ranges are visible and some of the most recent craters show prominent ray systems. These rays are the result of explosive impacts that ejected rock and soil up to 600 miles from the main crater. The most obvious radiate from the impact craters Tycho and Copernicus.

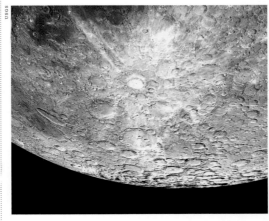

One of the Moon's most conspicuous craters is the 53-mile wide Tycho. It lies near the Moon's southern pole and with binoculars reveals a large system of bright rays and a dark halo.

A telescope reveals a wealth of fine detail on the Moon and the most outstanding views are right along the terminator. As sunrise progresses over each crater, its appearance changes rapidly. Tall mountains cast incredibly long shadows at first, gradually shortening as each day passes. As the Sun rises over a crater, the outer walls are illuminated first, followed by its peak, and finally its floor.

Thirty percent of the Moon's visible face is covered with dark flat areas of volcanic lava These are the maria and many are circular in

As it orbits Earth we observe phases of the Moon because we only see portions of the satellite illuminated by the Sun. As shown in this diagram (right), half of the Moon is always illuminated, but from our position on Earth we see it wax and wane throughout the month. The Moon completes a rotation in the same time it takes to revolve once completely around the Earth. This is why we always see the same side of the Moon. The "dark side" of the Moon is illuminated by the Sun every month, we just don't get a chance to see it.

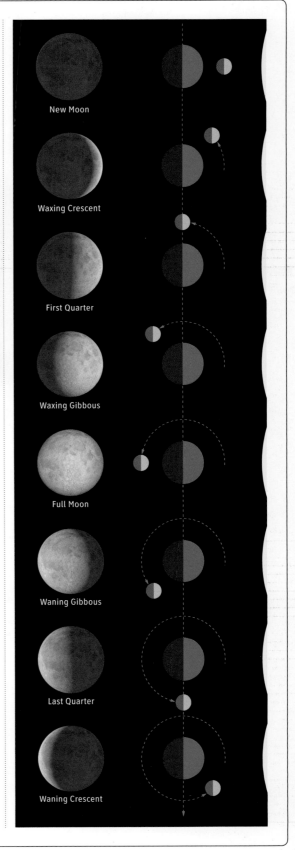

New Moon

Waxing Crescent

First Quarter

Waxing Gibbous

Full Moon

Waning Gibbous

Last Quarter

Waning Crescent

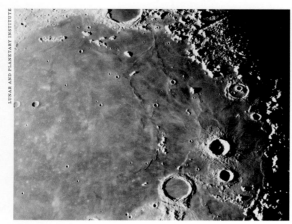

Shown here is part of the Mare Imbrium basin with the flat-floored crater, Plato, near the top. This mare is on view to us after the first quarter Moon.

The lunar Apennines, the most spectacular mountain region on the Moon, borders Mare Imbrium. The edge of the crater Archimedes is at the top. Located near the upper right is the location of the Apollo 15 landing site.

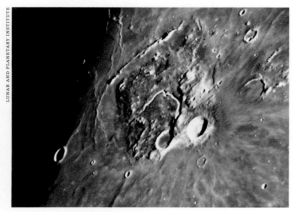

Aristarchus, one of the brightest features on the Moon, is shown here as it appears shortly after sunrise during a gibbous Moon. The sinuous Schröter's Valley winds across the elevated plateau.

appearance, such as Mare Crisium, Mare Serenitatis, and the huge Mare Imbrium. At least 3.2 billion years ago, the outer crust of the Moon was cracked by collisions with objects from space. Lava from within the Moon oozed out onto the surface, filling huge depressions left by the impacts. Craters formed from subsequent impacts, such as Copernicus, blew up huge quantities of lunar soil and ejected it miles across the lunar surface.

The surface of the Moon is a preserved history of the impact events of the distant past. Overlapping craters offer the opportunity to build a detailed history on a relative time scale of the intensity of the bombardment over many hundreds of millions of years. The Apollo missions returned to Earth with samples of the lunar soil and rocks allowing scientists to determine their age.

Some of the major craters become visible in the first week after new Moon. Look for the magnificent trio of Theophilus, Cyrillus, and Catherina on day six of a lunation. Three days later, Tycho catches sunlight. Soon after, brilliant rays appear to emanate from this crater that are easily visible in binoculars. To its north, almost midway down the terminator, three outstanding craters sit in high relief: Arzachel, Alphonsus, and Ptolemaeus are a trio of increasingly larger craters. The Apennines, the finest mountain chain on the Moon, borders Mare Imbrium in the far north. These majestic mountains rise three miles above the mare surface.

After ten days, the majestic crater Copernicus, rising dramatically out of the Ocean of Storms (Oceanus Procellarum), becomes visible. To its south, the well-worn walls of Gassendi also catch the Sun's rays. Two days later, two to three days before full Moon, Aristarchus is also visible at sunrise. Schröter's Valley, a dramatic collapsed lava tube, lies nearby.

At full Moon, the dramatic relief enhanced by shadows disappears, and the disk takes on a new appearance. Subtle shading across the mare plains is evident now. In the following two weeks, as the terminator traverses the Moon, the Sun sets over all the craters and mountains, creating a brand new perspective on every feature.

Astronaut Harrison Schmidt collects rock samples in the vicinity of a giant boulder during the Apollo 17 mission in December 1972. The lunar rover lies in the foreground.

LUNAR ECLIPSES

There are three types of lunar eclipses: total, partial, and penumbral. Each occurs about the same number of times during the year. Any eclipse of the Moon occurs only when the Moon is full and travels

MOON DATA	
Diameter	2,159 miles
Distance from Earth	Min: 221,463 miles Max: 252,719 miles
Orbital Period	27.32 days
Rotation Period	27.32 days
Synodic Month (Lunation)	29.53 days
Orbital Inclination	5° 32'24" (ecliptic)
Axial Tilt	1° 9'36" (ecliptic)
Orbital Inclination to Earth's Equator	18° 16'48"–28° 34'48"
Apparent diameter	Max: 33'31" Min: 29'22"
Albedo	0.12
Mass [1]	0.012
Density [2]	3.34
Surface Gravity [1]	0.0165
Escape Velocity	1.5 miles per second
First Manned Moon Landing	Apollo 11, July 20, 1969
Manned Landings	Apollos 11, 12, 14–17, 1969–1972

[1] Earth = 1
[2] Water = 1

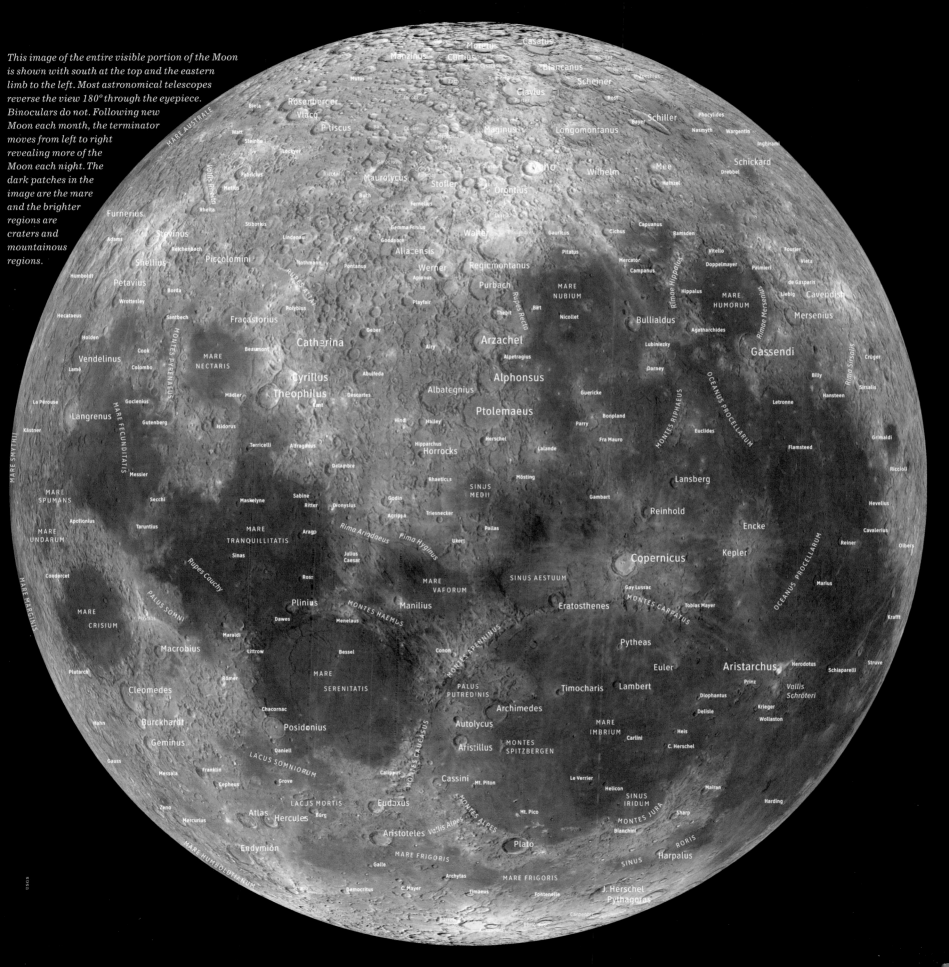

This image of the entire visible portion of the Moon is shown with south at the top and the eastern limb to the left. Most astronomical telescopes reverse the view 180° through the eyepiece. Binoculars do not. Following new Moon each month, the terminator moves from left to right revealing more of the Moon each night. The dark patches in the image are the mare and the brighter regions are craters and mountainous regions.

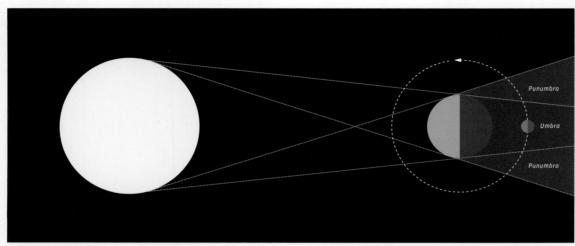

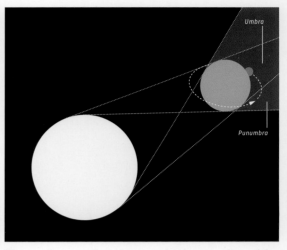

FRED ESPENAK/WWW.MRECLIPSE.COM

This composite image of a total lunar eclipse (center) shows the partial eclipse stages that occur before and after totality.

The two diagrams above (not to scale) show an eclipse of the Moon when it lies perfectly in the Earth's shadow made by the Sun. The darkest part of the shadow is called the umbra, and when the entire disk of the Moon lies within the umbra a total eclipse occurs. The area of partial shadow is called the penumbra.

THE DANJON SCALE

French astronomer André Danjon developed a scale to measure the relative brightness of the Moon during a total lunar eclipse. Cloud cover, weather conditions, recent volcanic eruptions, and other atmospheric conditions on Earth affect the brightness of an eclipse. Even during totality, some sunlight manages to reach the Moon and this is why it can be so beautiful to behold. Depending on conditions, the Moon can turn bright red or orange. Why? Because on its way to the Moon, brilliant white sunlight passes through the atmosphere of the Earth and blue light is filtered out, so only orange and red light reaches the Moon.

L=0 Very dark eclipse, Moon almost disappears.

L=1 Dark eclipse, gray or brown coloration, difficult to see details on Moon's surface.

L=2 Deep red or rust colored eclipse. The central shadow is dark and the outer edge is bright.

L=3 Brick red eclipse. The shadow becomes progressively brighter orange and yellowish toward the outer edges.

L=4 Very bright orange or reddish eclipse. Shadow has very bright rim, sometimes bluish in color.

TOTAL LUNAR ECLIPSES FROM 2007–2012

YEAR	DATE	TYPE	LOCATION
2007	Aug 28	Total	N. America except NE and S. America extreme east, the Pacific Ocean, Japan, New Zealand, Australasia
2008	Feb 21	Total	Africa, Europe, W. Asia, E. Arabia, Iceland, N. and S. America except SW Alaska
2010	Dec 21	Total	N. Europe, N. Asia, Iceland, N. and S. America, Hawaii, Pacific islands, New Zealand
2011	Jun 15	Total	S. America, Europe, Africa, Asia, Australia
2011	Dec 10	Total	Europe, E. Africa, Asia, Australia, Pacific, N. America

into the shadow of the Earth. A lunar eclipse does not occur at every full Moon because of the tilt of the lunar orbit relative to Earth's orbit by 5.32°. This tilt keeps the full Moon out of the shadow of the Earth. However, when the Moon's orbit and our own orbit align just so, an eclipse takes place.

The maximum duration of totality during a total eclipse is 1 hour 47 minutes. The entire eclipse including the partial phases can last more than four hours. The umbra, the dark shadow of the Earth, is typically more than two times the diameter of the Moon. Before the umbral shadow reaches the edge of the Moon, the limb of the Moon begins to darken. This is the penumbral shadow.

Partial eclipses occur when just a portion of the full Moon passes into an umbral shadow of the

Earth. Penumbral eclipses are extremely difficult to detect because there is only the slightest hint of shadow on the face of the Moon.

Total and partial eclipses of the Moon are visible to anyone on the night side of the Earth when they occur, whereas a total solar eclipse is visible from an area less than 169 miles wide. Unlike a solar eclipse, a lunar eclipse is also completely safe to view with the naked eye or optical instruments. Maps for locations to view lunar eclipses are available online at the NASA Eclipse Home Page.

Mars

OBSERVING MARS

Mars orbits the Sun in 687 Earth days and traces a more elliptical path than most planets. This orbit carries Mars through a widely varying distance from the Sun and from Earth, which consequently affects the red planet's visibility for observers. At perihelion, Mars lies 128.4 million miles from our central star. At aphelion Mars wanders 154.9 million miles from the Sun.

Every 780 days Mars lies directly opposite the Sun in our sky, and Earth and Mars line up. The time around opposition is the best time to view the red planet for two main reasons: Mars is closest to the Earth, and is visible all night. Its appearance, however, depends on whether Mars is near perihelion or aphelion. When Mars is at perihelion, such as in 2003, it lies just 35 million miles from Earth. Such perihelic oppositions occur every 15 to 17 years. At aphelion the closest Mars gets to Earth is a distant 60 million miles.

At a perihelic opposition, Mars outshines all other objects in the night sky except for the Moon and Venus. On these occasions Mars reaches magnitude −2.9. At a more distant opposition when Mars is near aphelion, it shines nearly as bright as Sirius, at magnitude −1.2. When Mars is faint it takes on a distinctly reddish hue, but as it brightens, the planet takes on a light orange color.

The most favorable period of visibility of Mars begins after its apparent diameter exceeds 10 arcseconds. When Mars is greater than this angular diameter, major surface features on Mars are visible in small telescopes.

The favorable observing period depends on Mars' distance from Earth and how fast it is moving. Mars moves faster along its orbital path at perihelion than at aphelion. If opposition occurs near perihelion, the favorable observing period for Mars lasts about 210 days. For aphelion, this period shrinks to 135 days.

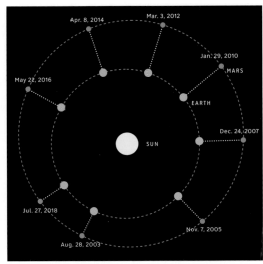

Oppositions of Mars 2003–2018. Due to its elliptical orbit, some oppositions are more favorable for observation because of the planet's proximity to Earth.

An apparition of Mars begins when the planet appears in the morning sky following conjunction on the far side of the Sun. This occurs 13–14 months before opposition. Earth is beginning its catch-up game, but due to the closeness of our orbital speeds—Earth is 18.5 miles per second and Mars is 15 miles per second—catching up with Mars takes some time.

Mars has the appearance of a dim "star" when it first appears in the morning sky. On each consecutive day at the first sign of dawn, Mars creeps higher and higher in the east. About three months before opposition, Mars rises at midnight and stands high in the south by daybreak.

Mars moves eastward relative to the background constellations during this period. About a month before opposition, this eastward motion stops. Earth has caught up with Mars and begins to overtake it. Like two cars passing each other on a highway going in the same direction, from the point of view of the observer, the slower car appears to move backwards. Mars does the same. As Earth begins to pass Mars on its faster, smaller orbit, Mars turns westward and each night appears progressively farther west against the background stars. This retrograde motion is typical of all the outer planets, but due to Mars' proximity to Earth, its retrograde loop is the most pronounced.

Following the retrograde motion of Mars, the main observing period enters a decline as the planet's disk shrinks in size. Over a period of many months Mars appears as a bright "star" sliding very slowly into evening twilight. Once it reaches conjunction with the Sun, occurring about a year after opposition, Mars is ready for its next close encounter with Earth.

After landing on Mars, January 4, 2004, the Spirit rover sent this panoramic view from the floor of Gusev Crater and the distant Columbia Hills. Note the rover's wheel marks to the right.

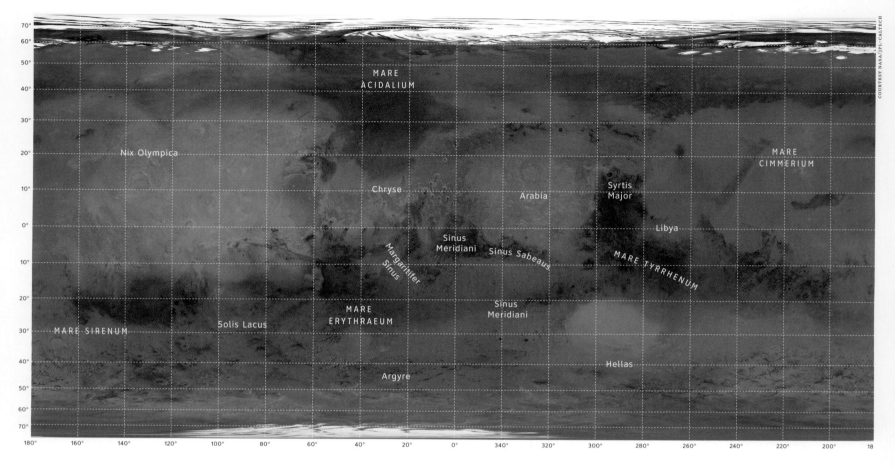

The map labels visible include:

MARE ACIDALIUM · Nix Olympica · MARE CIMMERIUM · Chryse · Arabia · Syrtis Major · Libya · Sinus Meridiani · Sinus Sabeaus · MARE TYRRHENUM · Margaritifer Sinus · MARE ERYTHRAEUM · Sinus Meridiani · Solis Lacus · MARE SIRENUM · Hellas · Argyre

This cylindrical projection map, created with data from the Jet Propulsion Laboratory, indicates major features, including icy polar regions.

PLANETARY FACTS

Mars, named after the Roman god of war, is the fourth planet in order of distance from the Sun. It orbits the Sun at a mean distance of 141.6 million miles, or 1.52 astronomical units. The outermost of the rocky planets, Mars has a diameter of 4,222 miles, which makes it about half the size of Earth. Although smaller, it has about the same land surface area as Earth since our planet is mostly covered by oceans.

Mars has two tiny moons, Phobos and Deimos. These moons skip completely around Mars in just 7.7 hours and 30.3 hours respectively. Although their magnitudes of +11.6 and +12.8 indicate medium-sized telescopes should be able to see them, the moons are so close to the brilliant globe of Mars that they are very difficult to spot.

When viewed from Earth, the surface of Mars is a brilliant orange disk dusted with dark brownish patches. The orange-red color of Mars is due to the iron oxide present on the surface. Brilliant white polar caps are visible that vary in size with the Martian seasons.

Surface temperatures on Mars vary with latitude and seasons. Near the equator, temperatures at the surface can reach 65°F, but a tall person standing on the surface would have a cold head, since six feet above the ground the temperature already drops to 15° F. At nighttime, the temperature drops to a frigid −130° F. This wide variation is partly due to the thin atmosphere on Mars.

Because Mars travels around the Sun in almost twice the time it takes Earth to do so, the Martian seasons are twice as long as ours. Seasonal variations are caused by the axial tilt of Mars of nearly 24°, very similar to Earth's tilt of 23.5°. Mars rotates in 24 hours 37 minutes.

MARS DATA

Diameter	4,222 miles
Distance from Sun	Max: 1.666 a.u. 154.86 mil. mi. Min: 1.381 a.u. 128.41 mil. mi.
Rotation Period	24 hours 37.4 minutes
Sidereal Period	687 days
Mean Synodic Period	780 days
Orbital Inclination	1° 50'59.4"
Inclination of Axis	23° 11'
Apparent Diameter	Max: 25.7" Min: 3.5"
Albedo	0.16
Mass [1]	0.1074
Density [2]	3.94
Surface Gravity [1]	0.38
Escape Velocity	3.1 miles per second

[1] (Earth = 1)
[2] (Water = 1)

MAJOR MARS FEATURES

FEATURE	LOCATION
Mare Acidalium	30°, +45°
Argyre	25°, -45°
Chryse	30°, +10°
Mare Cimmerium	220°, +20°
Mare Erythraeum	40°, -25°
Hellas	290°, -40°
Libya	270°, 0°
Margaritifer Sinus	25°, -10°
Nix Olympica	130°, +20°
Mare Sirenum	155°, -30°
Sinus Meridiani	0°, -5°
Sinus Sabeaus	340°, -8°
Solis Lacus	90°, -28°
Syrtis Major	290°, +10°

Global-wide dust storms can envelop Mars near opposition and obscure its features for observers. This double image shows a storm-free planet (left) and a dust-choked Mars (right).

Atmosphere. The Martian atmosphere, composed mostly of carbon dioxide with traces of nitrogen and argon, is very thin. The atmospheric pressure on the surface is equivalent to a height of 22 miles on Earth, a level high in our stratosphere. Thin as it is, the Martian air is powerful enough to lift huge dust storms. Occasionally these storms can envelop the entire planet, rendering any features invisible until the dust subsides.

Surface Features. Syrtis Major, a dark V-shaped feature, is the most prominent on the planet and varies in width with the Martian seasons. To its south is a bright circular region, sometimes mistaken for a polar cap, called Hellas. Spacecraft images of this region have revealed Hellas to be a deep impact basin. Dust activity is frequent in this region. Other well-known and prominent features include the sinuous Sinus Sabeaus, and the spider-like Solis Lacus (also known as Solis Planum)—the eye of Mars. Few of these Martian features relate to geological formations on Mars. Their seasonal changes in appearance are due to blowing dust exposing or covering rocky regions of the red planet.

White clouds are sometimes viewed near the limb or terminator of Mars, or associated with the polar caps. Future astronauts standing on

This image of the Martian surface clearly shows the large Schiaparelli crater. It is named for a famous Italian astronomer of the 19th and early 20th century.

Mars will see these white clouds set in a pinkish colored sky. The travel time to Mars for a manned mission would be at least seven months. The astronauts would have to stay on Mars until it was in a suitable position for a safe return to Earth, a period of at least a year, followed by another seven-month journey home. The entire trip would last about two Earth years.

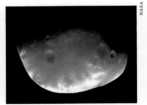

MARS SATELLITES

PHOBOS (LEFT)	
Diameter	16.8 × 13.7 × 11.2 mi.
Mean distance from Mars	5,825 mi.
Sidereal Period	7h 39.2m
Visual Magnitude	11.6

DEIMOS (RIGHT)	
Diameter	9.3 × 7.5 × 6.2 mi.
Mean distance from Mars	14,575 mi.
Sidereal Period	30h 17.9m
Visual Magnitude	12.8

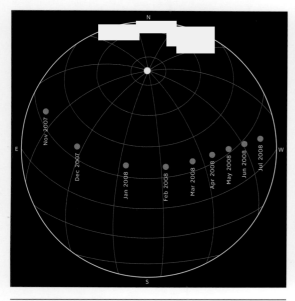

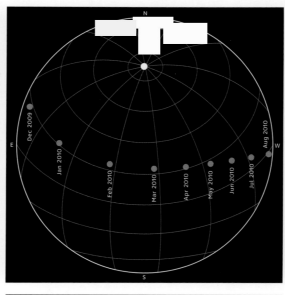

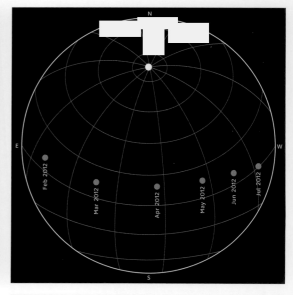

2007 OPPOSITION OF MARS

DATE	NOTES
Jun 4	At perihelion, 1.38 a.u. from the Sun.
Sep 25	Reaches 1.0 a.u. from Earth and shines at magnitude 0.0, in Taurus.
Oct 6	Reaches 10" apparent size, in Gemini.
Nov 16	Direct eastward motion halts, retrograde motion begins.
Nov 17	Shines at magnitude –1.0.
Nov 30	Reaches 15" apparent diameter.
Dec 18–19	Closest to Earth, 0.589 a.u. (54.75 million miles), 15.9" apparent diameter.
Dec 24	At opposition in Gemini, shining at magnitude –1.6.
Jan 7, 2008	Shrinks to 15" apparent diameter, in Taurus.
Jan 18	Fades to magnitude –1.0.
Feb 24	Shrinks to below 10" apparent diameter.
Feb 28	Recedes to more than 1.0 a.u, in Gemini.
May 13	At aphelion, 1.66 a.u. from the Sun.
Dec 5	In conjunction with the Sun.

2010 OPPOSITION OF MARS

DATE	NOTES
Nov 24, 2009	Reaches 1.0 a.u. from Earth in Cancer.
Nov 28	Shines at magnitude 0.0.
Dec 2	Reaches 10" apparent size, in Leo.
Dec 22	Direct eastward motion halts, retrograde motion begins, in Leo.
Jan 11, 2010	Shines at magnitude –1.0, in Cancer.
Jan 27–29	Closest to Earth, 0.664 a.u. (61,73 million miles), 14.1" apparent diameter, in Cancer.
Jan 29	At opposition in Cancer, shining at magnitude –1.3.
Feb 14	Fades to magnitude –1.0.
Mar 22	Shrinks to below 10" apparent diameter, in Cancer.
Mar 30	At aphelion, 1.66 a.u. from the Sun, and recedes to more than 1.0 a.u. from Earth.
Feb 4, 2011	In conjunction with the Sun.

2012 OPPOSITION OF MARS

DATE	NOTES
Jan 5	Mars reaches 1.0 a.u. from Earth (92,960,000 miles).
Jan 13	Mars reaches 10" apparent size, in Leo.
Jan 25	Direct eastward motion halts, retrograde motion begins in Virgo
Feb 15	Mars at aphelion, 1.666 a.u. from the Sun
Feb 19	Mars shines at magnitude –1.0, in Leo.
Mar 3	Mars at opposition in Leo, shining at magnitude –1.2.
Mar 5	Mars closest to Earth, 0.674 a.u. (62,655,000 miles), 13.9" apparent diameter, in Leo.
Mar 20	Mars fades to magnitude –1.0, in Leo.
Apr 14	Retrograde motion halts, resumes direct motion in Leo
Apr 30	Mars shrinks to below 10" apparent diameter, in Leo.
May 9	Mars recedes to more than 1.0 a.u.

In the illustrations above, the location of Mars on the celestial sphere is shown at 10:00 pm local time during opposition periods. Notice that near opposition dates, the position of Mars changes significantly from one month to the next, moving east to west. As Mars travels farther from the Earth after opposition, its position in the sky changes less.

Jupiter

OBSERVING JUPITER

Jupiter shows more detail through a telescope than any other planet and it's a fascinating place to explore from Earth. Jupiter's turbulent atmosphere, constantly churning and turning, reveals new features each time you look.

Typically the best opportunity to view a planet is the time around opposition. However, Jupiter is 12 times the diameter of the Earth and  the largest planet in the solar system; it's so large that any time it is visible it puts on a grand display. Its apparent size is always more than 30 arcseconds, and near opposition can reach up to almost 50 arcseconds.

Jupiter's atmosphere is split into dark belts and bright zones. They lie parallel to the planet's equator. Jupiter does not rotate as a solid object; it's a gaseous planet, known as one of the "gas giants," and its zones rotate at different rates. The two darkest bands are called the equatorial belts. A small telescope (60-mm diameter) will readily show these two main features of Jupiter's atmosphere and the four bright moons. Larger telescopes (6-inch and larger) are required for seeing smaller details between the equatorial belts, along with some of the finer features at higher latitudes.

The region between the equatorial belts rotates in a period of 9 hours 50 minutes, and is called the Equatorial Zone. It lies between the southern edge of the North Equatorial Belt and the northern edge of the South Equatorial Belt. The regions north and south of the equatorial belts rotate at the slightly slower speed of 9 hours 55 minutes. The regions connecting these dramatically different areas are very turbulent, generating swirls of dark material that change with each rotation of the planet.

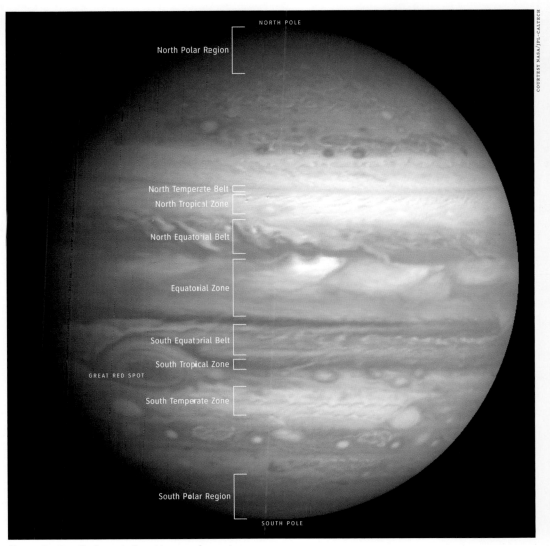

Above: Jupiter, the largest planet in our solar system, displays bands of high-velocity descending and ascending clouds across its turbulent outer atmosphere. Jupiter's clouds are composed of ammonia, hydrogen sulfide, and water. Small bright clouds near the Great Red Spot produce violent lightning and eastward-moving winds in its northern belts whip around the planet at speeds greater than 300 miles per hour.
Left: This fine telescopic view of Jupiter from a modest instrument reveals great details of the planet's atmosphere. Jupiter's size and brightness make it one of the most rewarding objects to view in the night sky.

Consider Earth, 12 times smaller, which rotates in 24 hours, and you get a sense of the breakneck speed of Jupiter's atmosphere. Features in the atmosphere parade past like we're watching a horse race from a grandstand. Careful observers of the planet will notice a change of position of prominent features within a 10 to 15 minute time interval. To gauge their motion, draw an imaginary line from its north pole through the center of the disk to the south pole. This represents the central meridian of the planet. Motion relative to this line becomes easy to spot with practice. Tracking these features with sketches or digital images enables the rotation period of each feature to be monitored.

The Great Red Spot, a three-century old storm system spanning almost three times Earth's diameter, sits on the southern edge of

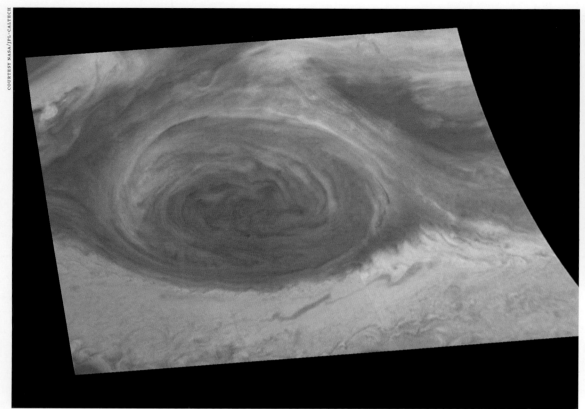

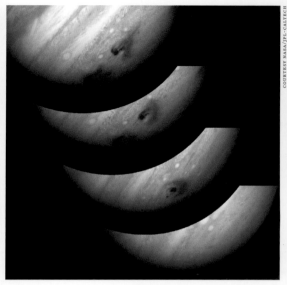

In 1994, Comet Shoemaker-Levy 9 broke apart under the gravitational influence of Jupiter. Its 22 pieces smashed into the atmosphere, producing dark clouds that were visible in small telescopes from Earth. This rare collision reminds us that planetary impacts do happen from time to time, and evidence of such impacts are found on the moons of Jupiter and most other planets and their satellites.

NASA's Galileo Orbiter captured this magnificent image of Jupiter's Great Red Spot in 1996. It is an anti-cyclonic storm, rotating counter-clockwise as it moves through the southern hemisphere of Jupiter. It has raged on for at least 300 years, gobbling up other storms it encounters in the atmosphere. Scientists think they have detected thunderheads along the edges of the storm that are filled with water.

the South Equatorial Belt. Since most astronomical telescopes invert the image, the southern belt will be the upper one as seen through the eyepiece. Its color often belies its name, since its pale pinkish hue is sometimes too subtle to be detected.

GALILEAN MOONS

Jupiter has a large number of moons, and four of them are very bright. If they happen to lie far enough from the planet they can be seen in binoculars. Small telescopes will show them easily. The Galilean moons, Io, Europa, Ganymede and Callisto, each perform a ritual dance each night, moving to and fro to the east and west of the planet. Sometimes the planet can hide one, two, or three of them at a time. The swiftest moon is Io, which takes 1.8 days to complete one orbit. Callisto takes nearly 17 days for an orbit.

Every time a moon passes in front or behind Jupiter, a transit or occultation occurs—such events occur almost nightly and are easily spotted

JUPITER DATA

Diameter	88,848 miles	
Distance from Sun	Max: 5.455 a.u.	506.9 mil. mi.
	Min: 4.950 a.u.	460.4 mil. mi.
Rotation Period	9h 50m–9h 55m	
Sidereal Period	11.86 years	
Mean Synodic Period	398.88 days	
Orbital Inclination	1° 18' 11"	
Inclination of Axis	3.1°	
Apparent Diameter	Max: 49"	
	Min: 30"	
Albedo	0.52	
Mass [1]	317.88	
Density [2]	1.32	
Surface Gravity [1]	2.69	
Escape Velocity	37.0 miles per second	
Satellites	63	

[1] (Earth = 1)
[2] (Water = 1)

in 60mm scopes. During transits, the moon passes in front of the planet, and its dark shadow is cast onto the atmosphere, where it is clearly visible moving slowly across the face of Jupiter.

During occultations, the moon disappears behind the limb of the planet. Under the right conditions, the Moon can be viewed passing into the shadow of Jupiter itself. This is called an eclipse. The huge shadow of the giant planet extends out to the left or right of the planet, depending on its relative location in the solar system to the Sun and Earth. Eclipses occur during the months before and after opposition. At opposition the shadow of Jupiter is precisely behind the planet's disk.

On rare occasions, all four moons will be hidden. One event occurs on May 21, 2008, lasting nearly 20 minutes beginning at 11:51 pm EDT. Another occurs on September 3, 2009, lasting for nearly two hours beginning at 12:44 am EDT.

PLANETARY FACTS

Jupiter is the largest planet in the solar system. It contains three times the mass of all the other planets put together, yet even so, it's only one-thousandth the mass of the Sun. Curiously, Jupiter radiates twice as much heat as it receives from the Sun. This indicates some internal source of heat, such as a hot core.

Jupiter orbits the Sun every 11.86 years. This places the planet opposite the Sun in our skies about every 13 months. Since there are 12 constellations along the ecliptic, Jupiter spends roughly one year in each one.

The dynamic atmosphere of the planet shows dark and light bands. The darker regions are warmer, as measured by infrared observations, and are deeper layers in Jupiter's atmosphere. The white clouds are cooler, higher features of the atmosphere. The Great Red Spot has fairly high cloud tops.

Jupiter is almost a mini-solar system in its own right. It has 63 moons we know of, but new ones, generally tiny lumps of rock caught in

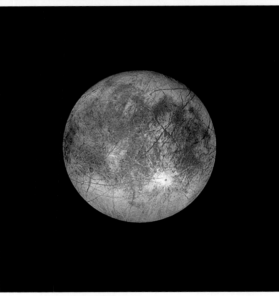

The four largest moons of Jupiter are known as the Galilean satellites, named for Galileo Galilei (1564–1642). In May of 1610 his book Starry Messenger was published in Venice announcing his discovery of many astronomical firsts including four tiny satellites of the planet Jupiter. The satellites are shown here in relative scale, Ganymede, (top left), Callisto, (top right), Io (bottom left), and Europa (bottom right).

Jupiter's huge gravitational field, are discovered each year.

Nearly 400 years ago, Galileo became the first person to see the four brightest moons of Jupiter. The motion of the moons around Jupiter made it clear to Galileo that the long-held belief that the Earth was the center of the solar system was wrong. The Galilean moons of Jupiter each have a fascinating story to tell. Their surfaces have been photographed at close range, first by the pair of Voyager spacecraft in 1979 and 1980, followed

by the three-ton Galileo spacecraft. It orbited the planet from 1995 until its fiery descent into the Jovian atmosphere on September 21, 2003. The controlled destruction of the spacecraft was to prevent it from striking the pristine surface of Europa at some time in the future. Europa is suspected of having an ocean of water under the surface ice.

Io, the innermost of the Galilean moons, is the most active volcanic object in the solar system. It has a diameter of 2,258 miles and orbits Jupiter in

1.8 days. The surface is covered with sulfur that shows up in different colors. Sulfur changes color depending on its temperature, from a pale yellow solid to an orange liquid that eventually turns pink or red at higher temperatures. Resurfacing of Io is caused by dozens of active volcanoes that spew sulfur to heights of 190 miles above the surface. Io's rotation is locked to its orbital period, so like Earth's moon, it keeps the same face pointing towards Jupiter. Every 3.5 days it passes Europa. The repeated gravitational pull from Jupiter and Europa generate heat inside Io, driving the volcanic processes.

Europa, the second of the Galilean moons, orbits Jupiter in 3.6 days. It's the smallest of the four moons, with a diameter of 1,948 miles. The surface is very smooth and has very few craters. At some time in the past, objects have struck every planet and moon in the solar system. If large craters ever existed on Europa, they have been obliterated by surface melting. The surface is criss-crossed with long, dark, linear features that resemble veins running across the retina in an eyeball. The moon is mainly water ice and the smoothness indicates melting that removes any high features. There is a fascinating possibility that there may be an ocean underneath the ice.

Europa is the target of a proposed space mission to land on the surface and penetrate the ice to see what lies beneath.

Ganymede is the largest of the Jovian moons, 3,273 miles across, making it larger than the planet Mercury. It has a varied surface of dark and light gray regions. Sixty percent of the surface is covered with areas of grooved terrain. Bright rays from crater impacts indicate it contains more water ice than surrounding areas. It is likely that the grooves are formed in a slushy surface as a water mixture seeps up through a weakened crust. There are a large number of craters that appear to become flattened with age. The darker terrain is far more heavily cratered, indicating they are of greater geological age than the lighter, grooved regions.

Callisto is the outermost of the four Galilean moons, and also the least dense. Its diameter is 2,986 miles, and contains large amounts of ice and relatively little rock. Its surface is very heavily cratered and is the darkest of the four moons. This suggests the surface has been preserved for a longer time than the other moons. Callisto orbits Jupiter in 16.7 days.

OPPOSITIONS OF JUPITER, 2007–12

YEAR	DATE	MAG.	APP. SIZE	CONST.
2007	Jun 5	-2.6	46"	Ophiuchus
2008	Jul 9	-2.7	47"	Sagittarius
2009	Aug 14	-2.9	49"	Capricornus
2010	Sep 21	-2.9	50"	Pisces
2011	Oct 29	-2.9	50"	Aries
2012	Dec 3	-2.8	48"	Taurus

CONJUNCTIONS OF JUPITER WITH OTHER PLANETS

From time to time, Jupiter appears in our skies fairly close to another planet. Such conjunctions are line-of-sight effects. In reality, the planets are very far apart. They provide a chance to see relative motion over a few days and interesting opportunities for photography.

JUPITER–MERCURY		NOTES
2007	Dec 20	*Too close to the Sun.*
2008	Dec 30	*Excellent conjunction, 1.2° apart in SW evening sky. Crescent Moon nearby on December 28 and 29.*
2009	Jan 18	*Too close to the Sun.*
2009	Feb 24	*Excellent morning conjunction, also with Mars in ESE before sunrise. Jupiter and Mercury 0.8° apart. March 1 Mercury and Mars close together.*
2010	Mar 7	*Too close to the Sun.*
2011	Mar 16	*Excellent evening pairing, 2.5° apart in the western sky.*
2011	May 10	*Beautiful morning conjunction, only 2.4° apart. Venus between the pair. Mars is 5° farther east but much fainter.*
2012	May 22	*Too close to the Sun.*

JUPITER–VENUS		NOTES
2008	Feb 1	*Spectacular morning conjunction before sunrise in the SE. Planets 0.6° apart and both very bright. Crescent Moon nearby on February 4.*
2008	Nov 30	*Spectacular conjunction in western sky after sunset. Planets 2° apart and both very bright. Crescent Moon stands below, and on December 1, above the pair.*
2010	Feb 16	*Very low in western sky and setting soon after the Sun. Only visible in bright twilight. 0.5° apart.*
2011	May 11	*Stunning morning pairing just 0.6° apart, with Mercury 1.5° south of Venus and Mars farther west.*
2012	Mar 15	*Spectacular conjunction in western sky after sunset. Planets 3° apart and both very bright.*

JUPITER–MARS		NOTES
2009	Feb 17	*Difficult early morning conjunction in ESE and in bright twilight. Planets 0.5° apart. Mars is faint. Mercury lies 7 degrees away.*
2011	May 1	*Best in binoculars, Jupiter easy but Mars faint, 0.4° to north in the eastern morning sky.*

JUPITER–SATURN		
None until 2020		

JUPITER–URANUS		NOTES
2010	Jun 6	*Uranus, at magnitude +5.9 and visible in binoculars, lies 0.5° north of Jupiter, in Pisces. Visible in the early morning sky in the east. Because of Jupiter's retrograde motion, it passes Uranus three times (see below).*
2010	Sep 22	*Uranus lies 0.9° north of Jupiter, in Pisces. Visible most of the night, a nearly full moon is nearby.*
2011	Jan 2	*Uranus lies 0.5° north of Jupiter, in Pisces. Visible in the western evening sky.*

JUPITER–NEPTUNE		NOTES
2009	May 25	*Neptune lies 0.4° north of Jupiter, in Capricornus. Neptune needs a telescope to view at magnitude +7.9. Visible in the SE, early morning. Because of Jupiter's retrograde motion, it passes Neptune three times (see below).*
2009	Jul 13	*Neptune lies 0.6° north of Jupiter. A bright star lies between Jupiter and Neptune. In the SE, late evening.*
2009	Dec 20	*Neptune lies 0.5° north of Jupiter. Crescent moon nearby in SW.*

Ref: Meeus, J., *Astronomical Tables of the Sun, Moon and Planets*

Saturn

OBSERVING SATURN

Saturn is the most beautiful planet in the solar system—a view through a telescope is breathtaking. The rings that encircle the globe are unique in the whole solar system and while Jupiter, Uranus, and Neptune have rings, they are very dark and not visible from Earth. Saturn's rings are bright, spectacular, and memorable.

Saturn is nearly the same size as Jupiter, but is twice as far from the Sun. Saturn's atmosphere is very dynamic, but its fine detail is hidden from Earthbound observers by an upper-level haze in its atmosphere.

Three different rings are visible through most telescopes. They are named simply A, B, and C. Ring B is the brightest. Between Ring A and Ring B is a dark division in the rings, almost 3,000 miles across, called the Cassini Division. Ring C is the dimmest of the three major rings. Spacecraft images of the rings have shown each of these three major rings to be actually hundreds of tiny ringlets. The individual ringlets are not visible in amateur telescopes on Earth, but appear as continuous sheets.

The planet and rings are tilted by 26° to the ecliptic. This means that from Earth we see

The outer edge of Saturn's majestic rings spans more than 170,000 miles. The rings are made up of millions of broken moons, cometary debris, ice, and fine dust particles. Surprisingly, most are only a few feet to several hundred feet deep. Their origin remains a mystery, though evidence indicates they are not stable, and may be regenerated and therefore only a few hundred million years old.

 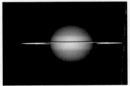  

Saturn is one of the finest sights in the night sky when viewed through a telescope. This detailed image (top) was captured using a webcam attached to a telescope and computer processed. Because of its axial tilt, the rings of Saturn appear in different positions to us on Earth over a period of years. Shown left to right are projected views from 2005, 2009, 2012, and 2017.

different views of the rings as Saturn orbits the Sun. The southern face of the rings has been visible from Earth since 1995. In September 2009 the rings will appear edge on—practically disappearing from view except though large professional telescopes. This is the only period that occultations and eclipses of the Saturnian moons take place. Following this ring plane crossing, the rings will appear to gradually widen, appearing at their widest in 2017.

When Saturn is a few months from opposition, the shadow of the planet can be seen falling on the far side of the rings. Before opposition, the planet's shadow on the rings lies to the west of the planet, and after opposition lies on the eastern side.

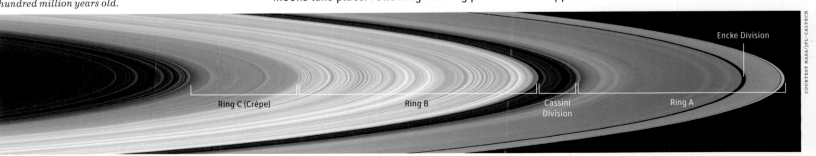

Ring C (Crépe) Ring B Cassini Division Ring A Encke Division

MOONS OF SATURN

Saturn has many bright moons that can be viewed from Earth. The brightest is Titan, a world in its own right, and the only moon in the solar system known to have a significant atmosphere. It orbits Saturn in a two-week period and is easy to see through a 60-mm telescope.

Other moons that orbit inside Titan's orbit, closer to Saturn, are Mimas, Enceladus, Tethys, Dione, and Rhea. Use a higher magnification that will help to reduce the glare of the planet and rings in order to glimpse these faint moons.

Orbiting outside Titan's orbit, Iapetus takes 79 days to complete one path around the ringed giant.

PLANETARY FACTS

Saturn is the sixth planet in the solar system and was the outermost planet known to the earliest civilizations. It's slightly smaller than Jupiter and ten times the diameter of Earth, spanning 74,900 miles at the equator. Like Jupiter, it has a smaller polar diameter of 67,000 miles. The equator bulges due to the fast rotational velocity. Saturn rotates once every 10 hours 39 minutes. Winds on the planet reach an amazing 1,800 miles per hour near the equator. Saturn has a hot interior and radiates more energy than it receives from the Sun.

Saturn contains about 75 percent hydrogen and 25 percent helium, similar to Jupiter, and curiously, to stars like our Sun. However, both Jupiter and Saturn are too small to become stars themselves. Both would need much more mass to create the superhot temperature and pressure for internal nuclear reactions. That's what keeps the stars burning brightly.

The density of Saturn is the lowest of all the planets. It is 0.7 grams per cubic centimeter, making it less dense than water. If you could find a container large enough, the planet would float in water.

COURTESY NASA/JPL–CALTECH

NASA/JPL/SPACE SCIENCE INSTITUTE

This image of Titan is a composite of four pictures taken by infrared cameras on board the Cassini spacecraft on March 31, 2005, from distances of approximately 91,000 to 81,000 miles. Infrared images are able to penetrate the thick atmosphere of Titan.

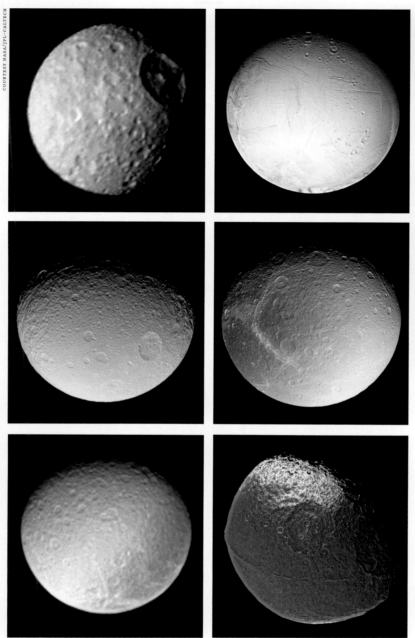

The system of satellites orbiting Saturn number 50 and new moons are discovered each year. Six of the larger moons are shown here (left to right, top to bottom) Mimas, Enceladus, Tethys, Dione, Rhea, and Iapetus.

SATURN DATA

Diameter	74,900 miles (equatorial)	
Rings	Out. dia. (ring A)	170,000 miles
	In. dia. (ring C)	92,600 miles
Distance from Sun	Max: 10.085 a.u.	933.9 mil. mi.
	Min: 9.014 a.u.	837.6 mil. mi.
Rotation Period	10h 39m	
Sidereal Period	29.46 years	
Mean Synodic Period	378.09 days	
Orbital Inclination	2° 29' 20"	
Inclination of Axis	26.7°	
Apparent Diameter	Max: 20"	
	Min: 14"	
Albedo	0.47	
Mass [1]	95.16	
Density [2]	0.69	
Surface Gravity [1]	0.916	
Escape Velocity	22.1 miles per second	
Satellites	56	

[1] (Earth = 1)

[2] (Water = 1)

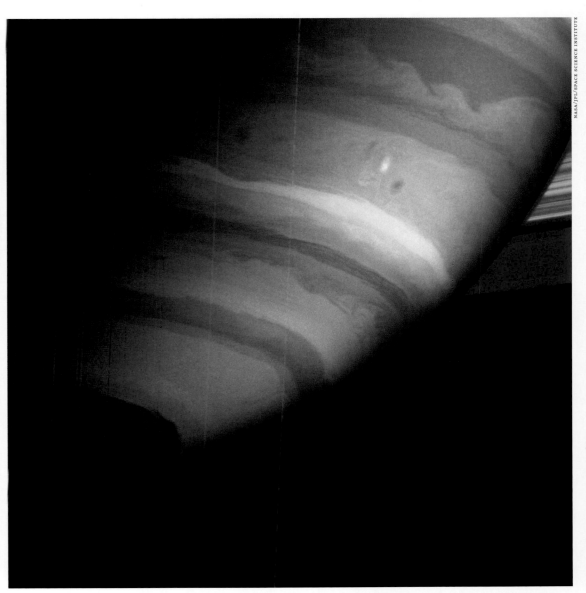

The Huygens probe returned this image from the surface of Titan on January 14, 2005. In the foreground are pebble-sized ice blocks. They are as hard as rock at below –289°F. The surface consists of a mixture of water and hydrocarbon ice. There is also evidence of erosion at the base of these objects, indicating some sort of fluvial activity.

The Cassini spacecraft's onboard near-infrared camera transmitted this glorious image of a portion of Saturn's southern hemisphere and the edge of its rings. A swirling red and orange area in the upper right of this image is known as the "Dragon Storm." It is a gigantic electrical thunderstorm and for several periods has produced radio emissions detected by Cassini. Thunderstorms in our own atmosphere produce similar radio waves.

EXPLORING SATURN

The first spacecraft to fly by Saturn was Pioneer 11 in late August 1979. The small spacecraft discovered a new ring around Saturn and paved the way for the follow-up missions.

Exploration by spacecraft of the Saturn system began in earnest during the early 1980s when the twin Voyager spacecraft performed fly-by missions. The dramatic images of Saturn and its retinue of moons provided scientists with unprecedented detail. Most intriguing, however, was Titan, Saturn's largest moon.

Titan is larger than the planet Mercury, with a diameter of 3,200 miles. It is shrouded in a thick atmosphere, and even Voyager's cameras could not penetrate the haze to see the surface. The die was cast that would lead to the development of the most exciting planetary mission ever undertaken—the Cassini-Huygens mission. A six-ton spacecraft carried the 703-pound Huygens probe destined for the surface of Titan, and the pair cruised to Saturn on a seven-year long journey, arriving in July 2004.

On January 14, 2005, the European Huygens probe made its successful descent to the surface of Titan. Combined with numerous fly-bys of Cassini during its main four-year orbital mission, Titan began to yield its secrets.

Titan has a largely nitrogen atmosphere with traces of methane and other gases. Earth is the only other object with a significant amount of nitrogen in its atmosphere and this has led scientists to believe that Titan is possibly an example of what the Earth was like before life developed. It's for this reason Titan gets so much attention.

The Huygens probe landed with a thud and a brief release of methane gas from the soil,

OPPOSITIONS OF SATURN, 2007–12

YEAR	DATE	MAG.	APP. SIZE	CONST.
2007	Feb 10	0.2	20.3"	Leo
2008	Feb 24	0.4	20.1"	Leo
2009	Mar 8	0.7	19.9"	Leo
2010	Mar 21	0.7	19.6"	Virgo
2011	Apr 3	0.6	19.4"	Virgo
2012	Apr 15	0.4	19.1"	Virgo

Saturn reached perihelion in 2003, and will reach aphelion in 2018.

indicating that the probe had landed in a muddy area. The light levels on the surface are comparable to bright twilight on Earth. River channels cut across the landscape, though the Huygens view showed them to be dry at present. The temperature on Titan is below -274°F where methane can exist as a gas or liquid. There is evidence of volcanic activity involving water ice and ammonia instead of lava.

Titan turns out to be the extraordinary world scientists thought it would be. The combination of the surface data from Huygens and the extensive mapping of the moon by Cassini gave scientists the facts they had hoped for and more.

The Cassini spacecraft discovered six new moons in its first few months in orbit, bringing Saturn's total retinue to 50. More are sure to be discovered each year.

COURTESY NASA/JPL-CALTECH

This image transmitted to Earth from the Cassini spacecraft in late 2005 reveals icy geysers shooting out from the south pole of Enceladus. Scientists believe the geysers form when liquid water erupts from beneath the surface of the moon and instantly freezes into giant plumes of water ice.

CONJUNCTIONS OF SATURN WITH OTHER PLANETS

From time to time, Saturn appears in our skies fairly close to another planet. Such "conjunctions" are line-of-sight effects. In reality the planets are very far apart. They provide a chance to see relative motion between two planets and offer interesting opportunities for photography.

SATURN–MERCURY	DATE	NOTES
2007	Aug 18	*Too near the Sun.*
2008	Aug 15	*Saturn 0.8° north of Mercury in bright twilight in the western evening sky. Venus 2.2° east of Saturn and easily visible.*
2009	Aug 18	*Saturn 3.6° north of Mercury in the western evening sky, in bright twilight.*
2009	Sep 20	*Too near the Sun.*
2009	Oct 8	*Saturn and Mercury 0.3° apart in the eastern morning sky. Venus about 5° above the pair.*
2010	Oct 8	*Too near the Sun.*
2011	Oct 7	*Too near the Sun.*
2012	Oct 6	*Briefly visible in WSW shortly after sunset, 4° apart. Very flat western horizon required.*

SATURN–VENUS		
2007	Jul 2	*Saturn 0.8° north of Venus in Leo, visible in the western evening sky.*
2007	Aug 9	*Too near the Sun*
2007	Oct 15	*Saturn 2.9° north of Venus in a dark early morning sky, in Leo.*
2008	Aug 13	*Saturn 0.5° from Venus in bright evening twilight, to the west. Mercury nearby.*
2009	Oct 13	*Low in the east, early morning, Saturn 0.5° north of Venus. Mercury nearby.*
2010	Aug 8	*Low in the west, Saturn 2.8° degrees north of Venus, in Virgo. A faint Mars about 4° east of Venus.*
2011	Sep 30	*Too near the Sun*
2012	Nov 27	*Spectacular conjunction only 0.75° apart in the morning sky, in Virgo. Mercury visible 11° below the pair.*

SATURN–MARS		
2008	Jul 10	*Saturn 0.7° north of Mars in Leo. Visible in western evening sky. Mercury visible nearby in Gemini.*
2010	Aug 1	*Saturn 1.8° north of Mars in the western evening sky in Virgo. Venus 8° away. Saturn, Mars, and Venus form triangle on August 5.*
2012	Aug 17	*Fine evening conjunction, 3° apart. Mars also 3° east of the bright star, Spica, in Virgo. Crescent Moon joins on August 21.*

SATURN–JUPITER		
None until 2020		

SATURN–URANUS		
None until 2032		

SATURN–NEPTUNE		
None until 2025		

Ref: Meeus, J., *Astronomical Tables of the Sun, Moon and Planets*

Uranus, Neptune, and Pluto

OBSERVING URANUS

Uranus glows as a dim light wandering slowly among the background stars. At its brightest, it reaches magnitude +5.5, making it easily visible in binoculars. The challenge is to spot which fifth-magnitude star is actually the planet, since there are so many stars close to the same luminosity. A telescopic view reveals the planet's bluish-green disk (spanning a mere 3.7 arcseconds) that distinguishes it from surrounding stars. Its disk is too small to make out any atmospheric detail, although some experienced observers have noted slight shading between the northern and southern hemispheres.

linked to this changing orientation, which may lead to small magnitude changes. Long-term changes of about 0.5 magnitudes have been recorded over the past few decades, perhaps as a result of changing cloud features. This is surprising because the Voyager spacecraft, in its 1986 flyby of the planet, recorded a bland atmosphere. In 2004, Uranus developed a new chain of cloud features at a high northern latitude that might form into a complete belt, changing the reflectivity of the planet.

The easiest time to spot Uranus is when it lies near a fairly bright star. Over a period of a few days, make a sketch or record a digital image of the field of view around the location of Uranus. The planet will reveal itself by moving relative to the background stars.

into Pisces in 2009, when the planet is also at aphelion. The following year, in 2010, Uranus is found in the same location in the sky as the bright planet, Jupiter, helping observers to locate it more easily. Each year Uranus makes a small retrograde loop nearly four degrees wide that lasts six months.

OBSERVING NEPTUNE

Neptune is similar in physical size to Uranus but lies an additional one billion miles farther away. At the staggering distance of 2.7 billion miles, Neptune subtends a tiny 2.4-arcsecond diameter. The brightest Neptune reaches is magnitude +7.8. You'll need a large pair of binoculars, say 20 × 80s, to pick out Neptune with any ease. At seven times fainter than

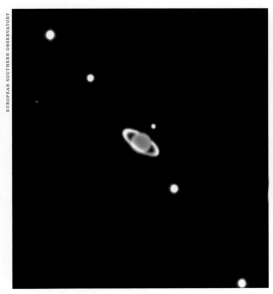

This radar telescope image of Uranus clearly shows its ring and six of its largest and brightest moons. Twenty-seven moons are known to circle Uranus.

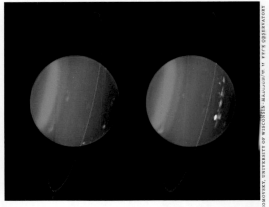

These side-by-side images of Uranus show relatively calm atmosphere (left) and turbulent cloud features (right) that have developed in its northern hemisphere over the past few years. Because of its axial tilt of 98°, its southern hemisphere appears eastern to us.

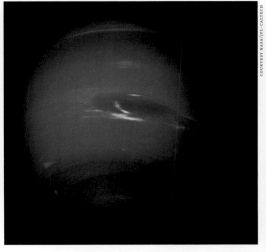

Voyager 2 transmitted data for this detailed image of Neptune. It clearly shows its equatorial Great Dark Spot and areas north and south with bright high-altitude cloud formations.

Uranus rotates on its side. Its north pole is tilted 98° to its orbit. The northern hemisphere is experiencing sunlight now for the first time in decades. In 2008, the planet's equator will be edge on to us and the southern pole will be pointing in the direction of orbital motion.

In recent years, large telescopes have revealed significant atmospheric changes

Uranus lies about 1.7 billion miles from Earth when it is at opposition. At this distance, it takes light over 2.5 hours to reach us. As you gaze at this distant planet, it's worth casting your mind back to 1781 when Sir William Herschel first spotted it. Prior to that date, only six planets were known, all visible without a telescope. Uranus represented the first telescopic discovery of a planet in our solar system.

Uranus is found in Aquarius until it moves

Uranus, simply finding the eighth planet is difficult. Telescopically, Neptune reveals very little, but its tiny disk can be distinguished from pinpoint stars, and some observers will detect its subtle bluish hue. Neptune lies in Capricornus through 2009, when it has a close conjunction with Jupiter.

In 2010, Neptune criss-crosses the Capricornus–Aquarius border during its retrograde loop. Triton, Neptune's largest moon, shines at magnitude +13.5, but lies very close to the glare of the planet.

OBSERVING PLUTO

Pluto represents the ultimate challenge for planetary viewers. Shining at magnitude +13.8, Pluto requires at least a 8-inch telescope to see from Earth. With many stars shining at a similar magnitude, the difficulty is identifying which object is Pluto. Digital images taken over consecutive nights will reveal its motion. Pluto crosses from Serpens Cauda into Sagittarius in 2007, where it will remain until 2023.

URANUS FACTS

Named for the ancient Greek god of the sky, Uranus is the seventh planet from the Sun. Uranus has been known for just over 200 years, and for most of that time little was known about it. We now know that its diameter is about four times larger than the Earth's. It's a gas giant, composed of hydrogen and helium, with some methane in its atmosphere. It takes a good human lifetime to orbit the Sun, once every 84 years.

In 1977, Uranus passed in front of a bright star, and during this occultation, starlight was blocked

URANUS DATA

Diameter	31,764 miles	
Distance from Sun	Max: 20.108 a.u.	1.87 bil. mi.
	Min: 18.329 a.u.	1.70 bil. mi.
Rotation Period	17.24 hours	
Sidereal Period	84.0 years	
Mean Synodic Period	369.66 days	
Orbital Inclination	0° 46'23"	
Inclination of Axis	97.86°	
Apparent Diameter	3.7"	
Albedo	0.5	
Mass[1]	14.54	
Density[2]	1.25	
Surface Gravity[1]	0.93	
Escape Velocity	13.1 miles per second	
Satellites	27	

[1] (Earth = 1)
[2] (Water = 1)

Miranda, with a diameter of 290 miles, is the smallest of the top five moons of Uranus. This Voyager 2 image shows its craggy surface of impact craters, ridges, and valleys. Its unusual geology suggests that it may have come apart, perhaps from multiple impacts, and reformed as many as five times.

out briefly at equal distances on either side of the planet. This marked the discovery of a ring system, and now 11 rings are known to exist.

The Voyager 2 spacecraft arrived at Uranus in January 1986, providing the first close-up views of the planet and its system of moons. Images of the planet itself proved very disappointing, showing a featureless, bland atmosphere.

Voyager revealed spectacular vistas of some of the more than 25 moons of Uranus. In particular, the jumbled chaos of Miranda showed that it had been broken apart by a large impact, only to be glued back together again by mutual gravity. Miranda's scarred landscape is unique in the solar system.

Oberon, Titania, and Umbriel showed few major geological features, but Ariel was criss-crossed by linear grooves and regions of ancient heavy cratering.

NEPTUNE FACTS

Neptune, the eighth planet from the Sun, and a twin of Uranus, was discovered in 1846. Named for the ancient Roman god of the sea, Neptune is similar in size to Uranus, with a diameter of 30,776 miles. The

This composite image of Uranus (top) taken by Voyager 2 approximates what the human eye would see from the vantage point of a spacecraft some 5.7 million miles away. The false color image (bottom) is greatly enhanced to show differences in its icy cold atmosphere composed almost entirely of methane gas.

main bulk of the planet consists of hydrogen and helium with traces of methane in its atmosphere. Only two moons were known before Voyager 2 visited the planet in 1989. Six additional moons were discovered during Voyager's historic flyby, and many more have been detected since that time.

After the featureless view of Uranus, Neptune surprised Voyager scientists by showing a dynamic atmosphere with a large dark spot reminiscent of the Great Red Spot on Jupiter.

Diameter	30,776 miles	
Distance from Sun	Max: 30.381 a.u.	2.83 bil. mi.
	Min: 29.840 a.u.	2.77 bil. mi.
Rotation Period	16.1 hours	
Sidereal Period	164.8 years	
Mean Synodic Period	367.49 days	
Orbital Inclination	1° 46'12"	
Inclination of Axis	29.56°	
Apparent Diameter	2.4"	
Albedo	0.41	
Mass [1]	17.15	
Density [2]	1.64	
Surface Gravity [1]	1.22	
Escape Velocity	15.3 miles per second	
Satellites	13	

[1] (Earth = 1)
[2] (Water = 1)

Voyager 2 confirmed the existence of four rings around Neptune. Some evidence regarding the possibility of rings had been observed for the first time in 1984.

Neptune's largest moon is Triton, which has a diameter of 1,681 miles. Following a flight over the pole of Neptune, Voyager 2 descended below its orbital plane to make a close encounter with the moon. Triton has an orbital inclination of 157°, with a retrograde orbit around the planet. Voyager 2 found an amazing world of active geysers, ice craters, and plumes of dark material blown

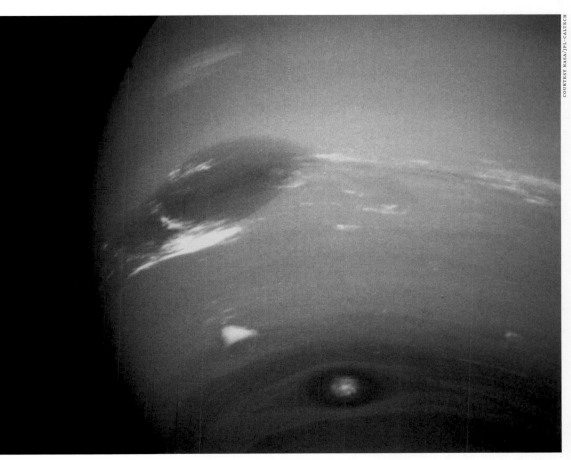

In this image, to the south of the Great Dark Spot of Neptune is a small bright feature. It's nicknamed "Scooter" by NASA scientists for its rapid eastern movement. Southeast of "Scooter" is Dark Spot 2 with a white central "eye."

downwind by an extremely rarified atmosphere of nitrogen. Active geysers constantly replenish the thin atmosphere.

PLUTO FACTS

Pluto is a tiny rocky object some 1,519 miles across and, along with its moon, Charon, orbits the Sun in 248 years. Pluto and Charon are tidally locked, keeping the same face towards each other during Charon's 6.4-day revolution about Pluto. This is also Pluto's rotation rate. Pluto's axis is highly inclined by 118°—it is tilted on its side.

Clyde Tombaugh discovered Pluto in 1930 while working at Arizona's Lowell Observatory. This distant icy rock became the ninth planet in our solar system. Over the years many other objects have been recorded in the outer solar system including Eris, an object larger than Pluto. This discovery along with other factors caused the International Astronomical Union in 2006 to reclassify Pluto as a "dwarf planet."

Voyager 2 discovered complete, but clumpy, rings around Neptune in its 1989 fly-by. The rings are made of very dark material whose precise composition is unknown.

PLUTO DATA		
Diameter	1,454 miles	
Distance from Sun	Max: 28.7 a.u.	2.67 bil. mi.
	Min: 49.3 a.u.	4.48 bil. mi.
Rotation Period	6.39 days (retrograde)	
Sidereal Period	247.68 years	
Mean Synodic Period	366.7 days	
Orbital Inclination	3° 23'24"	
Inclination of Axis	118.0°	
Apparent Diameter	0.1"	
Albedo	0.3	
Mass [1]	0.002	
Density [2]	1.8	
Surface Gravity [1]	0.05	
Escape Velocity	0.74 miles per second	
Satellites	3	

[1] (Earth = 1)
[2] (Water = 1)

This color image of Triton shows its fascinating landscape of nitrogen and methane ice and frost, and dark streaks from active geysers. Triton's surface is the coldest in the solar system at –391° F.

In 1994 NASA's Hubble Space Telescope captured this image of Pluto and its satellite Charon when they were 2.6 billion miles from Earth. It takes light approximately four hours to travel this distance. Light from the Sun reaches the Earth in just eight minutes. Hubble discovered two more moons of Pluto in 2005, called Nix and Hydra.

An extremely tenuous atmosphere of methane and other gases, first discovered in 1988, is expected to freeze out onto Pluto's surface as it recedes from the Sun between 2010 and 2020.

NASA's New Horizon mission spacecraft will arrive at Pluto in July 2015 to send back data.

CONJUNCTIONS WITH OTHER PLANETS

From time to time, Uranus, Neptune, and Pluto appear in our skies fairly close to another planet. Such conjunctions are line-of-sight effects. In reality, the planets are very far apart. They provide a chance to see the relative motion between two planets over a few days and offer interesting opportunities for photography. These fainter planets are never visible in twilight, so conjunctions with Mercury and Venus are ignored. No events occur with Pluto due to its high orbital inclination. Uranus and Neptune passed each other in 1993 and will not do so again until 2164.

URANUS–MARS		NOTES
2009	Apr 15	*Too near the Sun.*
2011	Apr 3	*Too near the Sun.*

URANUS–JUPITER		NOTES
2010	Jun 6	*Part of a triple conjunction with Jupiter. Both planets visible in binoculars or low power telescopic field of view in the early morning eastern sky. Uranus lies only 0.5° north of Jupiter. Crescent Moon lies 6° north of Jupiter.*
2010	Sep 22	*The second of a trio of conjunctions, Uranus lies 0.8° north of Jupiter. A bright moon is nearby. Both planets are at opposition on this date, and visible all night.*
2011	Jan 2	*Although outside our date range, this event is included because it is the third of a rare trio. Uranus lies 0.5° north of Jupiter in the evening sky in Pisces.*

URANUS–SATURN		
None		

NEPTUNE–MARS		NOTES
2007	Mar 25	*Too near the Sun.*
2009	Mar 8	*Too near the Sun.*

NEPTUNE–JUPITER		NOTES
2009	May 25	*First of a trio of conjunctions this year. Neptune lies 0.4° north of Jupiter in Capricornus in the morning sky.*
2009	Jul 13	*Neptune lies 0.6° north of Jupiter in Capricornus. The star μ Capricorni lies between the two planets. Visible nearly all night.*
2009	Dec 20	*In the SW evening sky near a crescent Moon, Neptune lies 0.5° north of Jupiter.*

NEPTUNE–SATURN		
None		

OPPOSITIONS OF NEPTUNE, 2007–12

YEAR	DATE	MAG.	APP. SZ.	CONST.
2007	Aug 13	7.8	2.4"	Capricornus
2008	Aug 15	7.8	2.4"	Capricornus
2009	Aug 17	7.8	2.4"	Capricornus
2010	Aug 20	7.8	2.4"	Capricornus/Aquarius
2011	Aug 22	7.8	2.4"	Aquarius
2012	Aug 24	7.8	2.4"	Aquarius

OPPOSITIONS OF URANUS, 2007–12

YEAR	DATE	MAG.	APP. SZ.	CONST.
2007	Sep 9	5.7	3.7"	Aquarius
2008	Sep 13	5.7	3.7"	Aquarius
2009	Sep 17	5.7	3.7"	Pisces
2010	Sep 21	5.7	3.7"	Pisces
2011	Sep 26	5.7	3.7"	Pisces
2012	Sep 29	5.7	3.7"	Pisces

OPPOSITIONS OF PLUTO, 2007–12

YEAR	DATE	MAG.	APP. SZ.	CONST.
2007	Jun 19	13.9	0.1"	Sagittarius
2008	Jun 20	13.9	0.1"	Sagittarius
2009	Jun 23	13.9	0.1"	Sagittarius
2010	Jun 25	14.0	0.1"	Sagittarius
2011	Jun 28	14.0	0.1"	Sagittarius
2012	Jun 29	14.0	0.1"	Sagittarius

January

The cold chill of a dark January night is illuminated by some spectacular stars and deep-sky objects. Soon after sunset, the brightest of the stellar canopy comes into view. Sirius, in Canis Major, the brightest star in the entire northern and southern skies, is first to appear. It is often found twinkling in multiple colors due to the prismatic effects of our turbulent atmosphere. Sirius lies low in the southeast at the time of January's chart.

A brilliant spread of stars continues with Procyon situated above the east-southeast horizon. To its right lies Orion's reddish star, Betelgeuse, located high above Sirius. Rigel, contrasting in color with Betelguese, lies in the lower right corner of Orion.

Three constellations gather nearly overhead. Gemini and its pair of bright stars, Castor and Pollux, lie due east. They're half-way up from the horizon to the overhead point called the zenith. A line of stars that runs to the southwest from Castor and Pollux forms the outline of the constellation.

Above Gemini is Auriga, the Charioteer. Auriga's most brilliant star, Capella, lies at the zenith at the time of January's chart. Seven additional stars, two close together, form the uneven hexagonal shape of Auriga. One of its stars, Alnath, is shared with Taurus, forming its upper horn. Taurus lies above and to the right of Orion. Aldebaran, its brightest star, lies among the Hyades, a beautiful V-shaped open cluster of stars. Nearby, M45, the Pleiades, is an elegant sight in binoculars. M45 is a more compact open cluster than the Hyades.

To the west of Orion, the sky seems empty of stars. A winding line of third- and fourth-magnitude stars forms the meandering Eridanus,

Auriga, the Charioteer, is shown here with its brightest star, Capella. The open clusters M36 and M38 can be seen in binoculars within the constellation.

the River. Farther west of Eridanus is Cetus, the Whale, reaching up to Taurus from the southwestern horizon. The baseball diamond group of four stars that outlines the Square of Pegasus lies above the western horizon. Markab is the lowest of the four in the sky, while the uppermost star is Alpheratz. The constellation of Pisces, the Fish, is a faint line of stars in an elongated V-shape that lies between Andromeda, Pegasus, and Cetus.

The northern sky is punctuated by many stars, most notably the leading pair of stars of Ursa Major, Dubhe and Merak. They are useful in pointing out the location of Polaris, the North Pole star. Extending an imaginary line from Merak through Dubhe and beyond, the next second-magnitude star you come to is Polaris. The pointers, as the pair are called, are climbing in the northeastern sky. The Big Dipper, Cassiopeia, Cepheus, and Draco circle the pole and never set. These circumpolar stars are always visible.

Polaris is the 48th brightest star in the sky. While its luminance is not impressive, its stature is. Polaris hardly moves. It remains due north every night of the year, while all the other stars appear to rotate around it. This illusion is caused by Earth's rotation on its axis.

The Orion Nebula, M42, is a spectacular nebula, a birthplace of stars. Hydrogen gas and dust mix in this celestial nursery about 1,500 light years from Earth. Through a telescope, faint tendrils of gas are easily visible, and Theta Orionis, found in the sword of Orion, reveals itself as four stars.

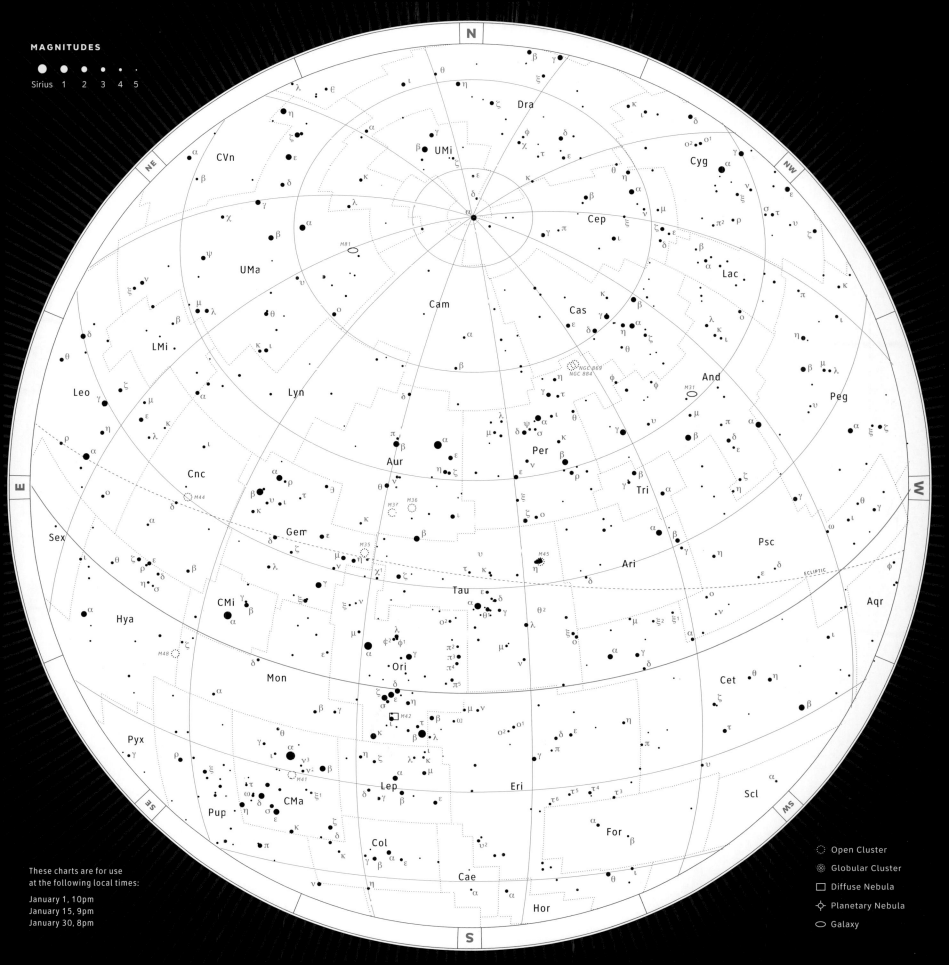

January

LIST OF CONSTELLATIONS

NAME	MEANING	ABBREV.
Andromeda	Princess	And
Aries	Ram	Ari
Auriga	Charioteer	Aur
Camelopardalis	Giraffe	Cam
Cancer	Crab	Cnc
Canis Major	Great Dog	CMa
Canis Minor	Little Dog	CMi
Cassiopeia	Queen	Cas
Caelum	Chisel	Cae
Cepheus	King	Cep
Cetus	Whale	Cet
Columba	Dove	Col
Draco	Dragon	Dra
Eridanus	River	Eri
Fornax	Lab. Furnace	For
Gemini	Twins	Gem
Hydra	Water Snake	Hya
Lacerta	Lizard	Lac
Leo	Lion	Leo
Leo Minor	Lion Cub	LMi
Lepus	Hare	Lep
Lynx	Lynx	Lyn
Monoceros	Unicorn	Mon
Orion	Hunter	Ori
Pegasus	Winged Horse	Peg
Perseus	Hero	Per
Pisces	Fish	Psc
Taurus	Bull	Tau
Triangulum	Triangle	Tri
Ursa Minor	Little Bear	UMi
Ursa Major	Great Bear	UMa

DEEP-SKY OBJECTS

These are the brightest of the deep-sky objects greater than magnitude 7 visible on this month's chart and are listed to the nearest whole magnitude. The visibility of deep-sky objects depends on their angular size. Galaxies and nebulae are extended objects and at magnitude 6 may still be difficult to make out because of low surface brightness.

OBJECT	LOCATION	TYPE	MAG.	COMMENTS
NCG 869 & NGC 884	Perseus	Open Cluster	4	The Double Cluster, two fine, rich, open clusters, best seen with binoculars.
M31	Andromeda	Galaxy	4	Andromeda Galaxy, a faint, hazy, elongated cloud, best viewed with binoculars or low-power telescope.
M33	Triangulum	Galaxy	6	An elusive object due to low surface brightness—best viewed in binoculars—very faint.
M35	Gemini	Open Cluster	5	Large open cluster, with 200 stars packed into an area the apparent size of the full moon.
M36	Auriga	Open Cluster	6	M36 and M37 are visible as fuzzy spots through binoculars and beautiful open star clusters when viewed through a small telescope.
M37	Auriga	Open Cluster	6	See M36.
M41	Canis Major	Open Cluster	5	A fine open cluster with stars of differing hues, a fine binocular object.
M42	Orion	Nebula	5	The Orion Nebula, the finest star-forming region on view, visible in binoculars as a fuzzy star, and spectacular in any telescope. The central four stars arranged in a trapezoid shape.
M44	Cancer	Open Cluster	3	The Beehive Cluster, also called Praesepe, a fine cluster in binoculars and telescope.
M45	Taurus	Open Cluster	2	The Pleiades, also Seven Sisters, a naked eye object, excellent in binoculars, with nearly 100 stars visible in small telescopes.
Algol	Perseus	Variable Star	2–3	Every 2–3 days Algol drops by nearly a magnitude due to a fainter orbiting companion eclipsing the brighter object.
γ Andromedae	Andromeda	Double star	2	An orange and blue star form an excellent color contrast, visible in small telescopes.

THE GREEK ALPHABET

LETTER	NAME	LETTER	NAME
α	alpha	ν	nu
β	beta	ξ	xi
γ	gamma	o	omicron
δ	delta	π	pi
ε	epsilon	ρ	rho
ζ	zeta	σ	sigma
η	eta	τ	tau
θ	theta	υ	upsilon
ι	iota	φ	phi
κ	kappa	χ	chi
λ	lambda	ψ	psi
μ	mu	ω	omega

BRIGHTEST STARS

NAME	DESIG.	MAG.	DISTANCE (LY)
Sirius	α CMa	−1.5	9
Capella	α Aur	0.1	42
Rigel	β Ori	0.1	773
Procyon	α CMi	0.4	11
Betelgeuse	α Ori	0.5	427
Aldebaran	α Tau	0.9	65
Pollux	β Gem	1.1	34
Deneb	α Cyg	1.3	3,228
Regulus	α Leo	1.4	78
Adhara	ε CMa	1.5	431
Bellatrix	γ Ori	1.6	243
Alnath	β Tau	1.7	131

February

As the Milky Way gently moves to the western half of the sky in February, it leaves behind an area in the eastern sky with far fewer stars. This area is a celestial window facing away from the obscuring dust and gas in the spiral arms of our galaxy and into intergalactic space. There are still a few stars within our own galaxy that we see, and these stars are now rising in the east.

Look to the northeast to find the Big Dipper, part of Ursa Major, the Great Bear. It's rising higher in the sky with each passing hour. The pointers, Dubhe and Merak, point down towards Polaris.

Using these pointers in the reverse direction, heading south, we find Leo, the Lion. This is one of the constellations whose shape actually resembles the figure it represents, a crouching lion. It's rising in the eastern sky, led by its brightest star, Regulus. A group of six stars shaped like a backwards question mark outlines the head of the Lion.

In the southeast, rising with Leo, is a faint string of stars anchored by the second-magnitude star Alphard. This is Hydra, the Water Snake. It wraps around the faint group called Sextans located just south of Leo.

Regulus is a first-magnitude star lying on the ecliptic. The ecliptic, the plane of our solar system, runs roughly east-west during February. Following the ecliptic higher in the sky, we find Cancer, the Crab.

Passing almost overhead is Castor and Pollux, the pair of bright stars in Gemini, the Twins. Gemini lies on the meridian, an imaginary line running north-south and directly overhead, through the zenith. Also near the meridian is Procyon, lying below Pollux. Lower in the south is the brightest star in the sky, Sirius, the Dog Star. M41, a fine open cluster of stars, is visible in binoculars south of Sirius.

The seven brightest stars of Ursa Major are shown here, forming the Big Dipper. The group is circumpolar, visible throughout the year. The second to last star in the handle is the naked eye double star, Mizar and Alcor.

M41 in Canis Major is an open cluster easily visible in binoculars.

Back to the ecliptic, over to the west and high in the sky is Taurus, the Bull. M45, the Pleiades, is a relatively nearby open cluster easily visible to the naked eye. Setting near the western horizon is Pisces. Its stars are so faint that most will disappear into the evening haze.

Orion dominates the southern sky with its stunning array of bright stars. Betelgeuse lies to the upper left of the constellation. It sports an orange hue, especially when compared to its bluish-white companion, Rigel, at the opposite corner of the constellation. Between the two bright stars lies a line of three stars close together. They represent the belt of Orion. The belt acts as a great signpost to other stars. Extending its line to the upper right leads to Aldebaran, and to the belt's lower left is Sirius.

Lepus, the Hare is a small grouping of stars below Orion. It's a small constellation with faint deep-sky objects and a double star, Gamma Leporis, within reach of binoculars.

Eridanus, the River, winds down towards the southwestern horizon, and adjacent to it is the last remnant of Cetus, the Whale, now diving gracefully below the horizon to the southwest.

Perseus, high in the northwest, and Cassiopeia, lying below it, dominate the northwestern sky. Just past the zenith lies Auriga, with its lead star, Capella, punctuating the dark sky overhead.

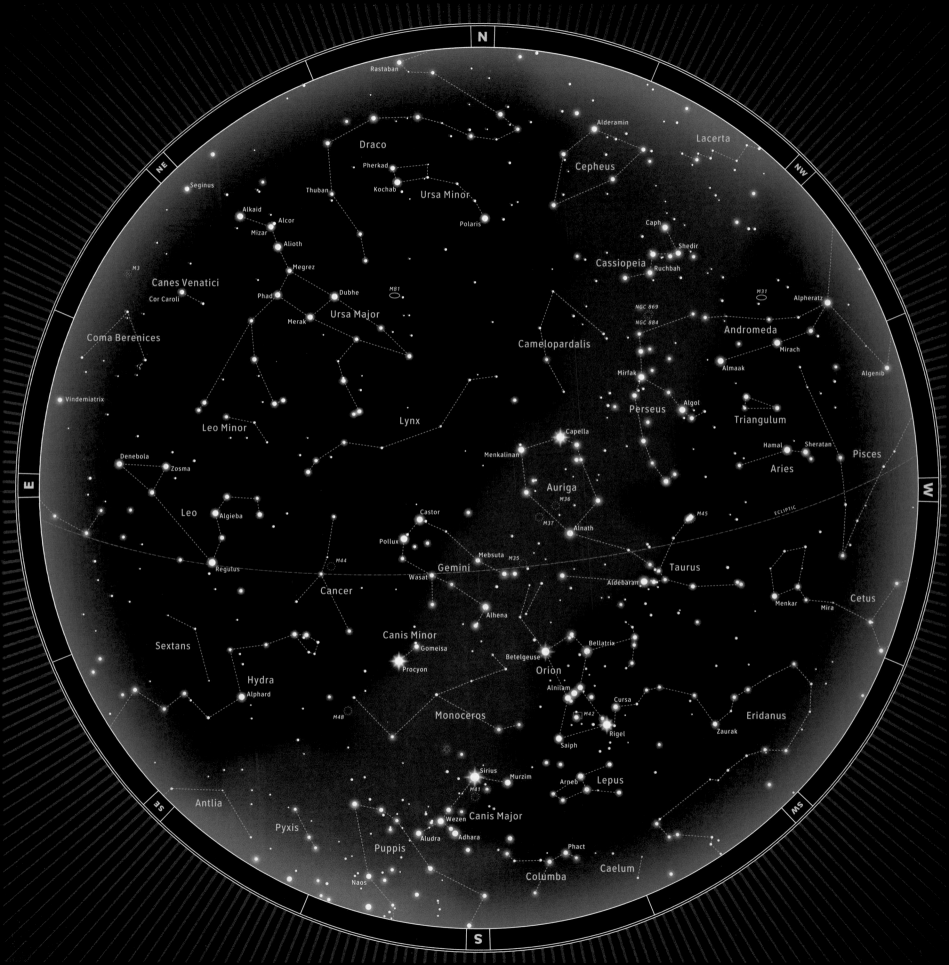

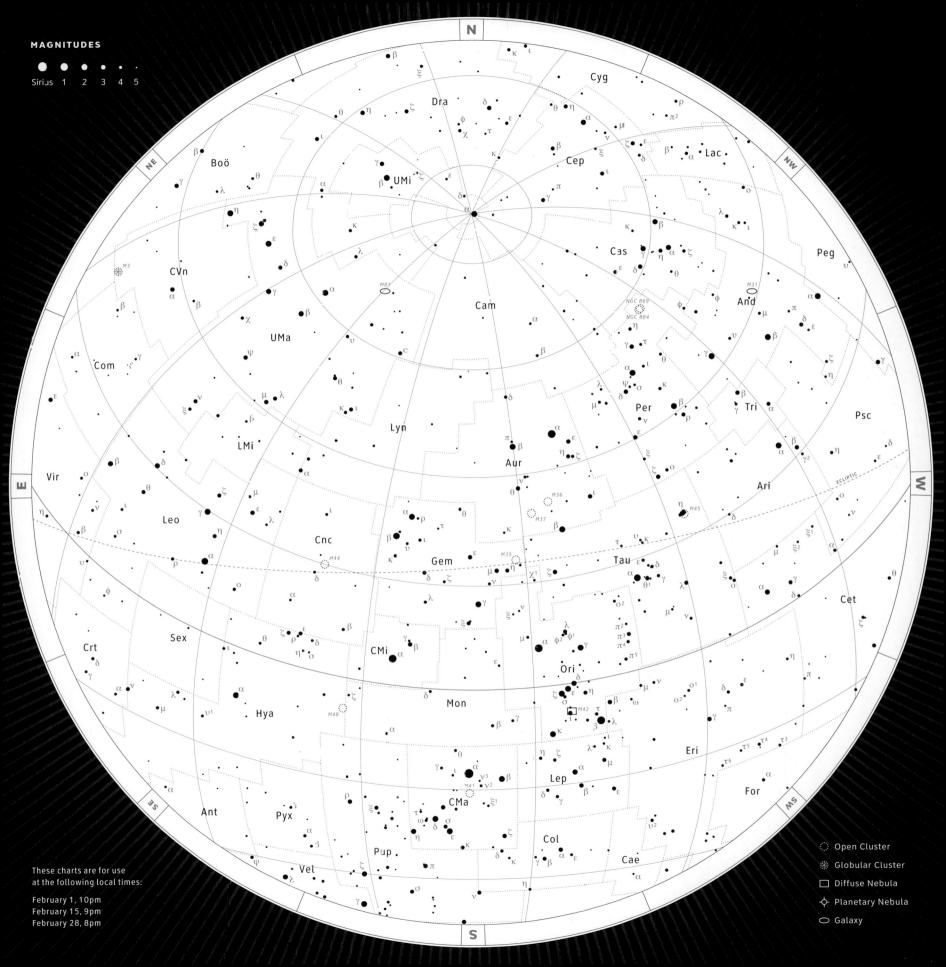

N

MAGNITUDES

Sirius 1 2 3 4 5

NE

NW

Dra

Cyg

Boö

UMi

Cep

Lac

Cas

Peg

CVn

M3

M81

And

M31

UMa

Cam

NGC 869
NGC 884

Com

Lyn

LMi

Per

Tri

Psc

Aur

Vir

Leo

Cnc

Gem

M36

M37

M45

Ari

ECLIPTIC

W

Tau

M35

Crt

Sex

CMi

M44

Mon

Ori

Cet

Hya

M48

M42

Eri

Lep

For

E

SE

Ant

Pyx

M41

CMa

Col

Cae

SW

Pup

Vel

These charts are for use
at the following local times:

February 1, 10pm
February 15, 9pm
February 28, 8pm

S

◌ Open Cluster

❋ Globular Cluster

▢ Diffuse Nebula

◇ Planetary Nebula

◯ Galaxy

February

LIST OF CONSTELLATIONS

NAME	MEANING	ABBREV.
Andromeda	Princess	And
Antlia	Air Pump	Ant
Aries	Ram	Ari
Auriga	Charioteer	Aur
Camelopardalis	Giraffe	Cam
Cancer	Crab	Cnc
Canes Venatici	Hunting Dogs	CVn
Canis Major	Great Dog	CMa
Canis Minor	Little Dog	CMi
Cassiopeia	Queen	Cas
Caelum	Chisel	Cae
Cepheus	King	Cep
Cetus	Whale	Cet
Columba	Dove	Col
Coma Berenices	Berenice's Hair	Com
Draco	Dragon	Dra
Eridanus	River	Eri
Gemini	Twins	Gem
Hydra	Water Snake	Hya
Lacerta	Lizard	Lac
Leo	Lion	Leo
Leo Minor	Lion Cub	LMi
Lepus	Hare	Lep
Lynx	Lynx	Lyn
Monoceros	Unicorn	Mon
Orion	Hunter	Ori
Perseus	Hero	Per
Pisces	Fish	Psc
Puppis	Stern	Pup
Pyxis	Compass	Pyx
Sextans	Sextant	Sex
Taurus	Bull	Tau
Triangulum	Triangle	Tri
Ursa Minor	Little Bear	UMi
Ursa Major	Great Bear	UMa

DEEP-SKY OBJECTS

These are the brightest of the deep-sky objects greater than magnitude 7 visible on this month's chart and are listed to the nearest whole magnitude. The visibility of deep-sky objects depends on their angular size. Galaxies and nebulae are extended objects and at magnitude 6 may still be difficult to make out because of low surface brightness.

OBJECT	LOCATION	TYPE	MAG.	COMMENTS
NCG 869 & NGC 884	Perseus	Open Cluster	4	*The Double Cluster, two fine, rich, open clusters, best seen with binoculars.*
M31	Andromeda	Galaxy	4	*Andromeda Galaxy, a faint, hazy, elongated cloud, best viewed with binoculars or low-power telescope.*
M35	Gemini	Open Cluster	5	*Large open cluster, with 200 stars packed into an area the apparent size of the full moon.*
M36	Auriga	Open Cluster	6	*M36 and M37 are visible as fuzzy spots through binoculars and beautiful open star clusters when viewed through a small telescope.*
M37	Auriga	Open Cluster	6	*See M36.*
M41	Canis Major	Open Cluster	5	*A fine open cluster with stars of differing hues, a fine binocular object.*
M42	Orion	Nebula	5	*The Orion Nebula, the finest star-forming region on view, visible in binoculars as a fuzzy star, and spectacular in any telescope. The central four stars arranged in a trapezoid shape.*
M44	Cancer	Open Cluster	3	*The Beehive Cluster, also called Praesepe, a fine cluster in binoculars and telescope.*
M45	Taurus	Open Cluster	2	*The Pleiades, also Seven Sisters, a naked eye object, excellent in binoculars, with nearly 100 stars visible in small telescopes.*
Algol	Perseus	Variable Star	2–3	*Every 2–3 days Algol drops by nearly a magnitude due to a fainter orbiting companion eclipsing the brighter object.*
γ Andromeda	Andromeda	Double star	2	*An orange and blue star form an excellent color contrast, visible in small telescopes.*
γ Leonis	Leo	Double Star	2	*A pair of yellowish bright stars, mag 2.4 and 3.6, visible in a telescope.*

THE GREEK ALPHABET

LETTER	NAME		LETTER	NAME
α	alpha		ν	nu
β	beta		ξ	xi
γ	gamma		ο	omicron
δ	delta		π	pi
ε	epsilon		ρ	rho
ζ	zeta		σ	sigma
η	eta		τ	tau
θ	theta		υ	upsilon
ι	iota		φ	phi
κ	kappa		χ	chi
λ	lambda		ψ	psi
μ	mu		ω	omega

BRIGHTEST STARS

NAME	DESIG.	MAG	DISTANCE (LY)
Sirius	α CMa	−1.5	9
Capella	α Aur	0.1	42
Rigel	β Ori	0.1	773
Procyon	α CMi	0.4	11
Betelgeuse	α Ori	0.5	427
Aldebaran	α Tau	0.9	65
Pollux	β Gem	1.1	34
Regulus	α Leo	1.4	78
Adhara	ε CMa	1.5	431
Bellatrix	γ Ori	1.6	243
Alnath	β Tau	1.7	131
Alnilam	ε Ori	1.7	1,342

March

This month the winter constellations are descending in the west, the weather is beginning to warm up, and the spring sky has arrived. While not as bright as the winter sky, the March sky is a window on the more distant universe.

The V-shape of Taurus points straight down to the western horizon. One of the most attractive sights of this month and next is watching a slim crescent Moon pass by M45, the Pleiades, set against the azure sky of the deepening twilight.

In the northwest, Aries is about to dip out of sight, and most people will not see it due to atmospheric haze or objects blocking the view. Triangulum and Andromeda are in the same situation. Perseus is higher in the northwest, with its rich collection of stars lying roughly parallel to the horizon.

Capella shines brightly to the upper right of Aldebaran. Three stars just below Capella form a neat little triangle and are called the "kids." Capella is a very close binary star comprising two yellow giant stars orbiting one another. The pair isn't visible in a typical telescope.

Orion leans over on its side above the southwestern horizon. The three belt stars lie horizontally, pointing to Aldebaran to their right and Sirius to their left. Puppis, the Stern, hugs the southern horizon but extends up as high as Sirius in the sky. This region contains many open star clusters worth scanning with binoculars.

Gemini and Canis Minor are just past the local meridian. To the east of them lies a dimmer region of sky, one full of hidden jewels. Cancer lies on the meridian, high in the south, and carries one of the finest open clusters in the sky, known variously as M44, the Beehive, and Praesepe.

Just below Cancer is a compact little group forming the head of Hydra, the Water Snake. This meandering constellation winds its way down to the southeastern horizon, skirting underneath Corvus and Crater. Crater represents a cup, and looks like it, while Corvus represents a crow, requiring considerably more imagination.

High in the southeast, Leo, the Lion, reigns. Regulus punctuates the backwards question mark shape of the Sickle, representing the head of the Lion. The rest of the constellation extends towards the east. Rising below Leo is Virgo and its brightest star, Spica, located very low in the east-southeast.

Cast your gaze far to the left of Spica to find Arcturus, rising in the east-northeast. You'll notice the color difference between these two stars. Spica is white, though Earth's atmosphere may cause twinkling that generates a spurious rainbow of colors. Arcturus, in Boötes, the Herdsman, has a distinctly orange color by comparison.

Ursa Major lies high above Boötes. Notice that the curved handle of the Big Dipper arcs down towards Arcturus, a useful way to locate the orange star. Nestled in the space between Arcturus and the Great Bear are two small constellations, Canes Venatici and Coma Berenices. Coma Berenices contains a cluster of faint stars, a wondrous sight in binoculars.

The region extending from the Dipper down to Virgo is rich with galaxies, best viewed when they are higher in the sky.

Top: The constellation of Taurus, the Bull. Aldebaran, the brightest star, is located near the V-shaped open cluster, the Hyades. Bottom: M3, a bright globular cluster in the constellation of Canes Venatici, lies 32,000 light years from Earth. This cluster contains half a million stars; their combined light makes it one of the brightest globulars in the sky.

March

LIST OF CONSTELLATIONS

NAME	MEANING	ABBREV.
Antlia	Air Pump	Ant
Aries	Ram	Ari
Auriga	Charioteer	Aur
Boötes	Herdsman	Boö
Camelopardalis	Giraffe	Cam
Cancer	Crab	Cnc
Canes Venatici	Hunting Dogs	CVn
Canis Major	Great Dog	CMa
Canis Minor	Little Dog	CMi
Cassiopeia	Queen	Cas
Cepheus	King	Cep
Cetus	Whale	Cet
Columba	Dove	Col
Coma Berenices	Berenice's Hair	Com
Corvus	Crow	Crv
Crater	Cup	Crt
Draco	Dragon	Dra
Eridanus	River	Eri
Gemini	Twins	Gem
Hydra	Water Snake	Hya
Leo	Lion	Leo
Leo Minor	Lion Cub	LMi
Lepus	Hare	Lep
Lynx	Lynx	Lyn
Monoceros	Unicorn	Mon
Orion	Hunter	Ori
Perseus	Hero	Per
Puppis	Stern	Pup
Pyxis	Compass	Pyx
Sextans	Sextant	Sex
Taurus	Bull	Tau
Triangulum	Triangle	Tri
Ursa Minor	Little Bear	UMi
Ursa Major	Great Bear	UMa
Vela	Sails	Vel
Virgo	Virgin	Vir

DEEP-SKY OBJECTS

These are the brightest of the deep-sky objects greater than magnitude 7 visible on this month's chart and are listed to the nearest whole magnitude. The visibility of deep-sky objects depends on their angular size. Galaxies and nebulae are extended objects and at magnitude 6 may still be difficult to make out because of low surface brightness.

OBJECT	LOCATION	TYPE	MAG.	COMMENTS
NCG 869 & NGC 884	Perseus	Open Cluster	4	*The Double Cluster, two fine, rich, open clusters, best seen with binoculars.*
M3	Canes Venatici	Globular Cluster	6	*A bright globular cluster located between Arcturus and Cor Caroli, an excellent telescopic object.*
M35	Gemini	Open Cluster	5	*Large open cluster, with 200 stars packed into an area the apparent size of the full moon.*
M36	Auriga	Open Cluster	6	*M36 and M37 are visible as fuzzy spots through binoculars and beautiful open star clusters when viewed through a small telescope.*
M37	Auriga	Open Cluster	6	*See M36 notes.*
M41	Canis Major	Open Cluster	5	*A fine open cluster with stars of differing hues, a fine binocular object.*
M42	Orion	Nebula	5	*The Orion Nebula, the finest star-forming region on view, visible in binoculars as a fuzzy star, and spectacular in any telescope. The central four stars arranged in a trapezoid shape.*
M44	Cancer	Open Cluster	3	*The Beehive Cluster, also called Praesepe, a fine cluster in binoculars and telescope.*
M45	Taurus	Open Cluster	2	*The Pleiades, also Seven Sisters, a naked eye object, excellent in binoculars, with nearly 100 stars visible in small telescopes.*
Algol	Perseus	Variable Star	2–3	*Every 2–3 days Algol drops by nearly a magnitude due to a fainter orbiting companion eclipsing the brighter object.*
γ Leonis	Leo	Double Star	2	*Also called Algeiba, a fine telescopic, orange-yellow, double star with a close third-magnitude companion.*
α CVn	Canes Venatici	Double Star	3	*Also called Cor Caroli, a fine telescopic double star with a fifth-magnitude companion.*

THE GREEK ALPHABET

LETTER	NAME	LETTER	NAME
α	alpha	ν	nu
β	beta	ξ	xi
γ	gamma	o	omicron
δ	delta	π	pi
ε	epsilon	ρ	rho
ζ	zeta	σ	sigma
η	eta	τ	tau
θ	theta	υ	upsilon
ι	iota	φ	phi
κ	kappa	χ	chi
λ	lambda	ψ	psi
μ	mu	ω	omega

BRIGHTEST STARS

NAME	DESIG.	MAG.	DISTANCE (LY)
Sirius	α CMa	−1.5	9
Arcturus	α Boö	0.0	37
Capella	α Aur	0.1	42
Rigel	β Ori	0.1	773
Procyon	α CMi	0.4	11
Betelgeuse	α Ori	0.5	427
Aldebaran	α Tau	0.9	65
Spica	α Vir	1.0	262
Pollux	β Gem	1.1	34
Regulus	α Leo	1.4	78
Adhara	ε CMa	1.5	431
Bellatrix	γ Ori	1.6	243

April

In April, the stars of winter are scattered around the western horizon like diamond dust glowing in the twilight. Sunset comes later each day this month, shortening the nighttime hours to less than eight. Taurus and Orion both set at nearly the same time, Orion in the direction of due west and Taurus farther around the horizon to the north. In the northwest, the stars of Perseus hug the horizon, watched over by Capella, Auriga's brightest star, higher above the horizon to the west-northwest.

Since January, the faint winter Milky Way has slowly moved to the west and now lies along the western horizon. The summer Milky Way is preparing to rise above the eastern horizon. Our view straight up into the sky is directly out of the plane of our galaxy. The stars we see are relative neighbors. Between the stars, we gaze out directly into intergalactic space. Galaxies are very distant, and very faint, resembling faint puffs of cloud in telescopes. Yet this region of sky, from the Big Dipper high overhead all the way through Virgo, is the realm of distant galaxies. Most are below ninth magnitude and require at least a 4-inch telescope to observe.

The Dipper lies almost directly overhead, and the pointers now aim straight down to the north, pointing at Polaris, the Polar Star. From the Dipper, circling around in a northeasterly direction around Polaris, we find Draco, the Dragon. Low to the north is Cepheus, and adjacent to it you'll find the W-shape of Cassiopeia. These are some of the circumpolar constellations and they never set from latitude 40° North.

In the southern sky, Leo crosses the local meridian, the imaginary north-south line across the sky. After rising in the east, this position is the highest it ever gets in the sky. Regulus, its brightest star, is easy to see. Move two stars up along the sickle shape of stars to

M41, in Canis Major, is a bright open cluster lying below Sirius, visible in binoculars. The cluster is 25 light years across and lies 2,100 light years from Earth.

its north and you'll find Algieba. This is a nice telescopic double star.

Leading the nose of Leo, to its west, is Cancer, the Crab. The constellation is faint and lies north of a line connecting Regulus and Procyon. A faint pair of stars in the center of the group is a good locator for M44, a good open cluster for binoculars.

The head of Hydra, the Water Snake, lies below Cancer. You can trace a faint line of stars all the way across to the southeastern horizon, making Hydra the largest constellation in the sky.

In the southeastern sky, Virgo, a faint sprawling constellation led by its brightest member, Spica, is rising. It's the second largest constellation in the sky, after Hydra. Northwest of Spica, the star Porrima is a good third-magnitude telescopic double star. Both stars are of equal brightness.

In the east and northeast, Boötes, Corona Borealis, and Hercules are rising. Arcturus shines brightly above the eastern horizon. Very low to the northeast, the brilliant star, Vega, in Lyra rises higher each hour, the first hint of the summer sky returning once again.

A spectacular spiral galaxy, M81 is found in Ursa Major. It is shown here with its neighbor in the sky, M82, which is undergoing a rapid burst of star formation. Both galaxies lie within the same low-power telescopic field of view.

The twin stars of Gemini, Castor and Pollux, sit like a pair of interstellar headlights high above the western horizon. Follow a curved line from the Twins down to the southwest. First you'll come across the bright solitary star, Procyon, in Canis Minor, the Little Dog. Far below it, hugging the horizon, is Sirius, twinkling violently after the strong air currents of a warm spring day subside.

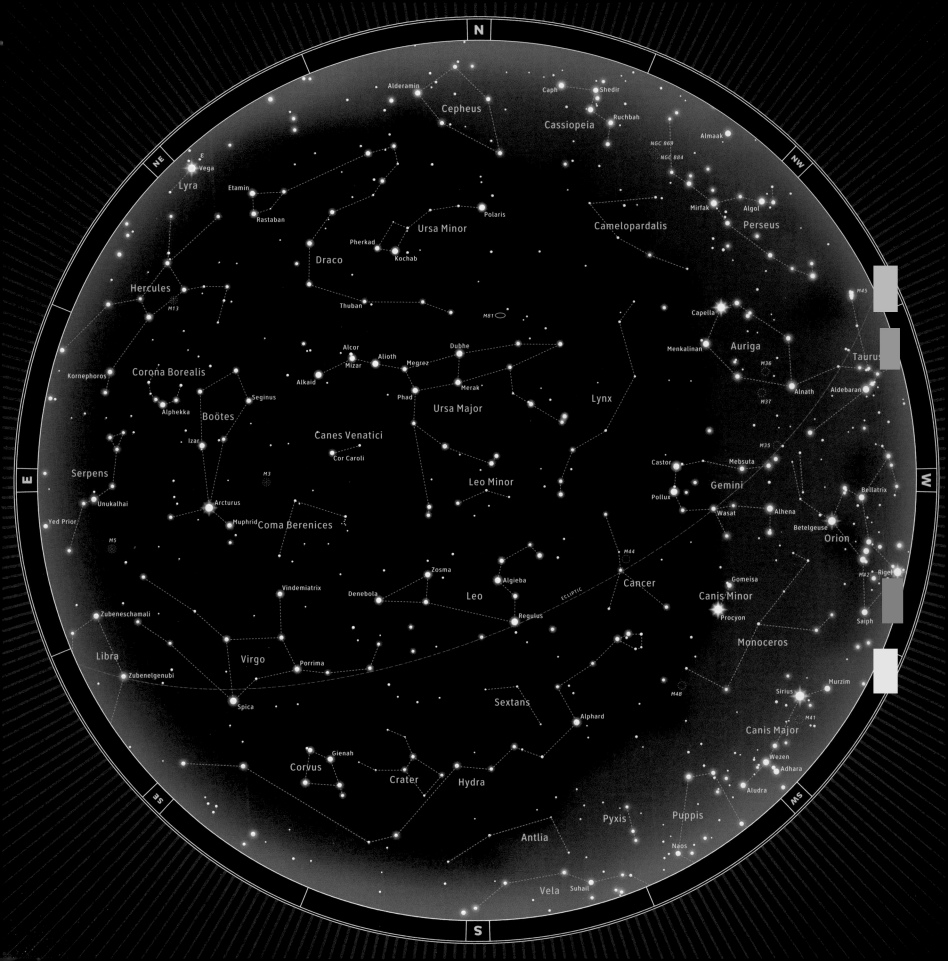

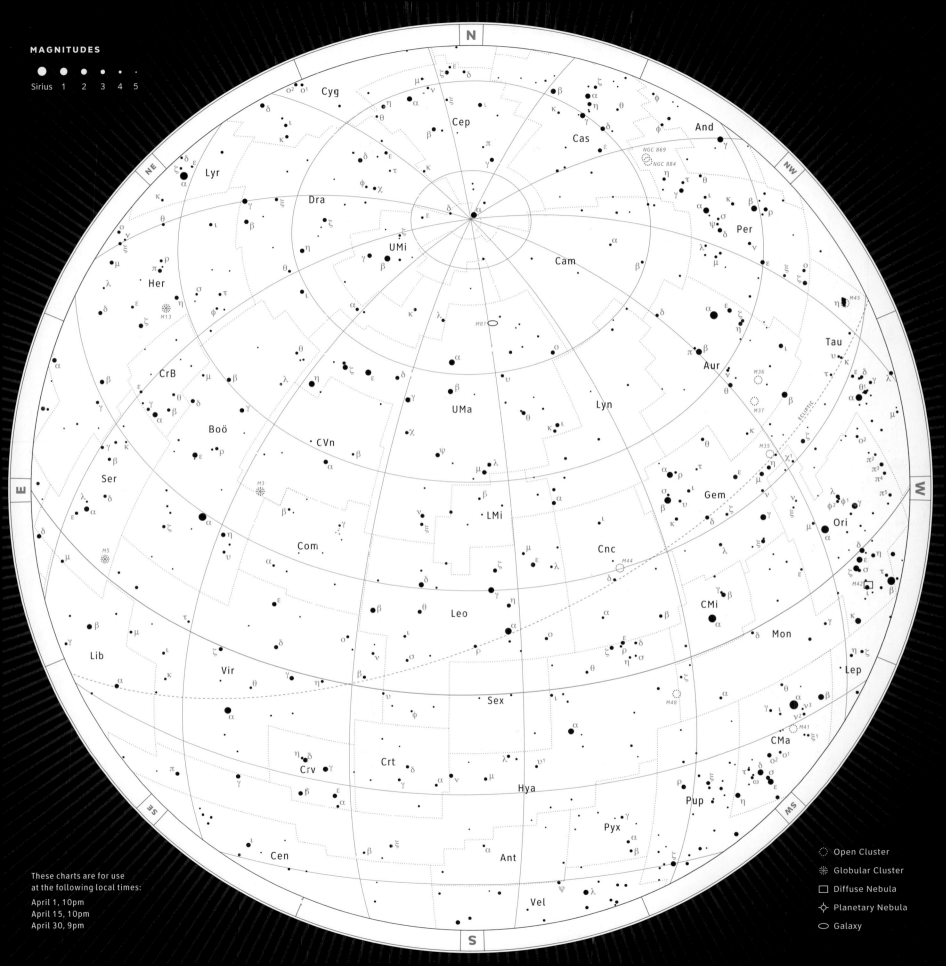

MAGNITUDES

Sirius 1 2 3 4 5

N

NE

NW

E

W

SE

SW

S

Cyg
Cep
Cas
And
Lyr
Dra
NGC 869
NGC 884
Per
UMi
Cam
Tau
Her
Aur
M45
CrB
M13
Lyn
M36
UMa
M37
ECLIPTIC
Boö
CVn
Gem
M35
Ser
M3
LMi
Cnc
Ori
Com
M44
M5
Leo
CMi
M42
Mon
Lib
Vir
Lep
Sex
M48
Crt
Pup
CMa
M41
Hya
Crv
Cen
Ant
Pyx
Vel

These charts are for use
at the following local times:

April 1, 10pm
April 15, 10pm
April 30, 9pm

○ Open Cluster
⊛ Globular Cluster
▢ Diffuse Nebula
◇ Planetary Nebula
◯ Galaxy

April

LIST OF CONSTELLATIONS

NAME	MEANING	ABBREV.
Antlia	Air Pump	Ant
Auriga	Charioteer	Aur
Boötes	Herdsman	Boö
Camelopardalis	Giraffe	Cam
Cancer	Crab	Cnc
Canes Venatici	Hunting Dogs	CVn
Canis Major	Great Dog	CMa
Canis Minor	Little Dog	CMi
Cassiopeia	Queen	Cas
Cepheus	King	Cep
Coma Berenices	Berenice's Hair	Com
Corona Borealis	North. Crown	CrB
Corvus	Crow	Crv
Crater	Cup	Crt
Draco	Dragon	Dra
Gemini	Twins	Gem
Hercules	Hercules	Her
Hydra	Water Snake	Hya
Leo	Lion	Leo
Leo Minor	Lion Cub	LMi
Libra	Scales	Lib
Lynx	Lynx	Lyn
Lyra	Harp	Lyr
Monoceros	Unicorn	Mon
Orion	Hunter	Ori
Perseus	Hero	Per
Puppis	The Stern	Pup
Pyxis	Marin. Comp.	Pyx
Serpens	Serpent	Ser
Sextans	Sextant	Sex
Taurus	Bull	Tau
Ursa Minor	Little Bear	UMi
Ursa Major	Great Bear	UMa
Vela	Sails	Vel
Virgo	Virgin	Vir

DEEP-SKY OBJECTS

These are the brightest of the deep-sky objects greater than magnitude 7 visible on this month's chart and are listed to the nearest whole magnitude. The visibility of deep-sky objects depends on their angular size. Galaxies and nebulae are extended objects and at magnitude 6 may still be difficult to make out because of low surface brightness.

OBJECT	LOCATION	TYPE	MAG.	COMMENTS
M3	Canes Venatici	Globular Cluster	6	A bright globular cluster located between Arcturus and Cor Caroli, an excellent telescopic object.
M35	Gemini	Open Cluster	5	Large open cluster, with 200 stars packed into an area the apparent size of the full moon.
M36	Auriga	Open Cluster	6	M36 and M37 are visible as fuzzy spots through binoculars and beautiful open star clusters when viewed through a small telescope.
M37	Auriga	Open Cluster	6	See M36.
M44	Cancer	Open Cluster	3	The Beehive Cluster, also called Praesepe, a handsome cluster in binoculars and telescope.
M45	Taurus	Open Cluster	2	The Pleiades, also Seven Sisters, a naked eye object, excellent in binoculars, with nearly 100 stars visible in small telescopes.
M48	Hydra	Open Cluster	6	A fine open cluster containing about 50 stars visible in binoculars
M81	Ursa Major	Galaxy	7	Spiral galaxy visible in telescopes at low magnification, with a fainter edge-on neighboring galaxy, M82, lying within one degree.
γ Leonis	Leo	Double Star	2	Also called Algieba, a fine telescopic, orange-yellow, double star with a close third-magnitude companion.
α CVn	Canes Venatici	Double Star	3	Also called Cor Caroli, a good telescopic double star with a fifth- magnitude companion.
Porrima	Virgo	Double Star	3	A pair of stars of equal brightness and color, easily split in small telescopes.
Izar	Boötes	Double star	2	One of the finest telescopic double stars in the sky, consists of a pair of orange and blue stars.

THE GREEK ALPHABET

LETTER	NAME	LETTER	NAME
α	alpha	ν	nu
β	beta	ξ	xi
γ	gamma	o	omicron
δ	delta	π	pi
ε	epsilon	ρ	rho
ζ	zeta	σ	sigma
η	eta	τ	tau
θ	theta	υ	upsilon
ι	iota	φ	phi
κ	kappa	χ	chi
λ	lambda	ψ	psi
μ	mu	ω	omega

BRIGHTEST STARS

NAME	DESIG.	MAG.	DISTANCE (LY)
Sirius	α CMa	−1.5	9
Arcturus	α Boö	0.0	37
Vega	α Lyr	0.0	25
Capella	α Aur	0.1	42
Rigel	β Ori	0.1	773
Procyon	α CMi	0.4	11
Betelgeuse	α Ori	0.5	427
Aldebaran	α Tau	0.9	65
Spica	α Vir	1.0	262
Pollux	β Gem	1.1	34
Regulus	α Leo	1.4	78
Adhara	ε CMa	1.5	431

May

Gemini and Canis Minor are the last vestiges of the winter constellations remaining in May's early evening sky near the western horizon. Aside from the occasional planet making an appearance, Procyon is the brightest star in the western sky. Above Procyon, the faint group Cancer is descending, becoming difficult to pick out in the evening haze. Leo appears to be on the downward leg of a leap across the sky as it begins its descent in the southwestern sky.

Hydra stretches from the western sky near Procyon, along the horizon to a point below Spica in the south-southeast. Cradled above its line of stars are Corvus and Crater, two small constellations now placed due south in May.

Above this pair of constellations, we find Virgo. Spica, and its neighboring star to the northwest, Porrima, are the brightest pair of stars in the constellation. A line of stars north and west of Porrima borders an area that contains dozens of faint galaxies. All of the galaxies are of ninth magnitude and below, placing them within reach of a 4-inch or

The Sombrero Galaxy, M104, as revealed by the Hubble Space Telescope. This unusual galaxy lies 65 million light years away in the constellation of Virgo. A thick dust lane is silhouetted against the bright glowing halo of the galaxy. This dust lane is visible in small telescopes.

6-inch telescope. These faint smudges of light represent the light of millions of stars from galaxies millions of light years away in the Virgo supercluster of galaxies.

Higher along the sky's north-south dividing line (meridian) lies Coma Berenices, an unremarkable group, yet home to the fine globular cluster that is listed third in Messier's famous catalog, M3. Scan your binoculars across this region—dozens of faint stars will be visible. Directly overhead lies Cor Caroli, the brightest of a pair of stars that marks the group Canes Venatici.

Moving through the overhead point (zenith) and turning to the north, you'll find Ursa Major, the Great Bear. The seven brightest stars, called the Big Dipper, make a useful signpost to other constellations. Notice that a line from Megrez through Dubhe points to the northwest where Capella, in Auriga, is located. Use the pointers Dubhe and Merak in reverse to guide you to Regulus, in Leo, to the south. Follow the arc of the handle of the Big Dipper to Arcturus, the brightest star in Boötes, the Herdsman. Continue the arc farther south to find Spica.

The lower eastern third of the sky contains new constellations rising higher

with each passing hour. The dim grouping of Libra, the Scales, is followed closely by the head of Scorpius. The bright star above the southeastern horizon is Antares. Spanning the eastern horizon, almost reaching Antares, is the dim grouping of Ophiuchus. In the east-northeast, Hercules is rising higher in the sky, carrying with it the spectacular globular cluster M13. Nestled between Hercules and Boötes is an attractive curve of stars called Corona Borealis, the Northern Crown.

The northeastern horizon provides evidence of the arrival of the summer constellations, led by Vega, in Lyra, the Harp. Low in the sky, with its long neck stretched parallel to the horizon, is the majestic constellation Cygnus, the Swan. The brighter parts of the Milky Way run through this group, but haze will keep it hidden until it rises higher in the sky later in the night.

Facing due north, the W-shape of Cassiopeia is evident, reaching its lowest point in the sky for the year. Cepheus has begun its slow rise in the north-northeast, and above it Draco, the Dragon, curls around Ursa Minor, the Little Bear, and home to Polaris, the North Pole star.

M5 is a stunning globular cluster when viewed through a telescope. A quarter of a million stars combine to make it one of the brightest globular clusters in the northern hemisphere.

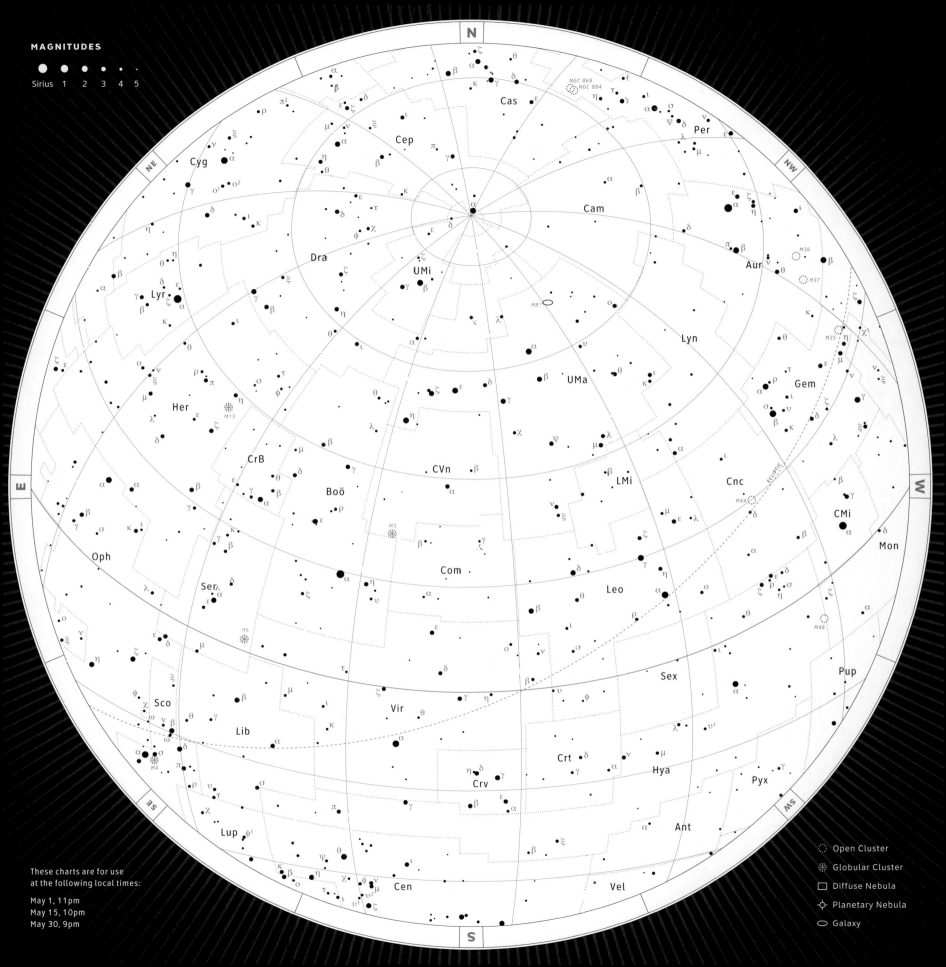

MAGNITUDES

Sirius 1 2 3 4 5

N

NE

NW

E

W

SE

MS

S

Cas
Cep
Cam
Per
Aur
Gem
Lyn
CMi
Mon
Cnc
LMi
UMa
CVn
Leo
Com
Sex
Crt
Hya
Pyx
Ant
Vel
Pup
Dra
UMi
Cyg
Lyr
Her
CrB
Boö
Ser
Oph
Sco
Lib
Vir
Crv
Cen
Lup

NGC 869
NGC 884
M36
M37
M35
M44
M48
M81
M3
M13
M5
M4

ECLIPTIC

These charts are for use
at the following local times:

May 1, 11pm
May 15, 10pm
May 30, 9pm

◌ Open Cluster
✸ Globular Cluster
▢ Diffuse Nebula
◈ Planetary Nebula
◯ Galaxy

May

LIST OF CONSTELLATIONS

NAME	MEANING	ABBREV.
Antlia	Air Pump	Ant
Auriga	Charioteer	Aur
Boötes	Herdsman	Boö
Camelopardalis	Giraffe	Cam
Cancer	Crab	Cnc
Canes Venatici	Hunting Dogs	CVn
Canis Minor	Little Dog	CMi
Cassiopeia	Queen	Cas
Cepheus	King	Cep
Centaurus	Centaur	Cen
Coma Berenices	Berenice's Hair	Com
Corona Borealis	North. Crown	CrB
Corvus	Crow	Crv
Crater	Cup	Crt
Cygnus	Swan	Cyg
Draco	Dragon	Dra
Gemini	Twins	Gem
Hercules	Hercules	Her
Hydra	Water Snake	Hya
Leo	Lion	Leo
Leo Minor	Lion Cub	LMi
Libra	Scales	Lib
Lynx	Lynx	Lyn
Lyra	Harp	Lyr
Monoceros	Unicorn	Mon
Ophiuchus	Serpent Bearer	Oph
Perseus	Hero	Per
Pyxis	Compass	Pyx
Scorpius	Scorpion	Sco
Serpens	Serpent	Ser
Sextans	Sextant	Sex
Ursa Minor	Little Bear	UMi
Ursa Major	Great Bear	UMa
Virgo	Virgin	Vir

DEEP-SKY OBJECTS

These are the brightest of the deep-sky objects greater than magnitude 7 visible on this month's chart and are listed to the nearest whole magnitude. The visibility of deep-sky objects depends on their angular size. Galaxies and nebulae are extended objects and at magnitude 6 may still be difficult to make out because of low surface brightness.

OBJECT	LOCATION	TYPE	MAG.	COMMENTS
M3	Canes Venatici	Globular Cluster	6	A bright globular cluster located between Arcturus and Cor Caroli, an excellent telescopic object.
M5	Serpens	Globular Cluster	6	A bright globular cluster in a sparse region of sky, an excellent telescopic object.
M13	Hercules	Globular Cluster	5	The brightest northern hemisphere globular, visible in binoculars and best through telescopes.
M44	Cancer	Open Cluster	3	The Beehive Cluster, also called Praesepe, a fine cluster in binoculars and telescope.
M48	Hydra	Open Cluster	6	A good open cluster containing about 50 stars visible in binoculars.
M81	Ursa Major	Galaxy	7	Spiral galaxy visible in telescopes at low magnification, with a fainter edge-on neighboring galaxy, M82, lying within one degree.
γ Leonis	Leo	Double Star	2	Also called Algieba, a lovely telescopic, orange-yellow double star with a close third-magnitude companion.
α CVn	Canes Venatici	Double Star	3	Also called Cor Caroli, a fine telescopic double star with a fifth-magnitude companion.
Porrima	Virgo	Double Star	3	A handsome pair of stars of equal brightness and color, easily split in small telescopes.
Izar	Boötes	Double star	2	One of the finest telescopic double stars in the sky, consists of a pair of orange and blue stars.

THE GREEK ALPHABET

LETTER	NAME	LETTER	NAME
α	alpha	ν	nu
β	beta	ξ	xi
γ	gamma	o	omicron
δ	delta	π	pi
ε	epsilon	ρ	rho
ζ	zeta	σ	sigma
η	eta	τ	tau
θ	theta	υ	upsilon
ι	iota	φ	phi
κ	kappa	χ	chi
λ	lambda	ψ	psi
μ	mu	ω	omega

BRIGHTEST STARS

NAME	DESIG.	MAG.	DISTANCE (LY)
Arcturus	α Boö	0.0	37
Vega	α Lyr	0.0	25
Capella	α Aur	0.1	42
Procyon	α CMi	0.4	11
Antares	α Sco	1.0	604
Spica	α Vir	1.0	262
Pollux	β Gem	1.1	34
Deneb	α Cyg	1.3	3,228
Regulus	α Leo	1.4	78
Alnath	β Tau	1.7	131
Alioth	ε UMa	1.8	81
Mirfak	α Per	1.8	592

June

June, the start of summer, has the shortest nights of the year. Observing time is reduced to only five hours of darkness per night. To the west, right after the late evening sunset, Regulus hangs above the horizon. Hydra, the Water Snake, slithers along the horizon from west to south, if visible at all due to haze. Virgo lies above the southwestern horizon. Porrima, the second brightest star in the constellation, is a fine telescopic double star.

High above the southern horizon, Arcturus dominates the sky, shining like an orange beacon. Its constellation, Boötes, the Herdsman, extends to the north. Izar, also called Epsilon Boötis, is a superb telescopic double star with vivid contrasting colors of orange and blue. It's located almost due north of Arcturus. Adjacent to Boötes' eastern side lies the small curved group of stars representing Corona Borealis, the Northern Crown. A little farther to the east is Hercules. Most of its stars are quite faint. Four stars represent the body of Hercules. The bright globular cluster, M13, a spectacular telescopic object, lies near the star on the northwestern side of the group.

Ophiuchus, the 11th largest constellation in the sky, is a sparse group that contains three bright globular clusters. Two of them, M10 and M12, are within easy reach of small telescopes. Ophiuchus represents the Serpent Bearer, and holds the Serpent, the only constellation in the sky split into two parts. The head of the Serpent, Serpens Caput, lies on the western side of Ophiuchus, extending upwards towards Hercules. The tail, Serpens Cauda, extends from Ophiuchus to the eastern side and reaches into the Milky Way.

Scorpius, the Scorpion, rises to the south of Ophiuchus. Antares, its brightest star, shines with an orange hue not unlike the planet Mars. Antares is called the "rival of Mars" and thus the origin of its name, anti-Ares.

Ahead of Scorpius, to the west, is the small constellation of Libra, the Scales. Alpha Librae, also called Zubenelgenubi, is an easy binocular double star. Iota Librae, located in the center of the constellation, is an attractive telescopic double star.

M10, a globular cluster in Ophiuchus, lies 14,300 light years away and is visible in binoculars.

Rising due east is Aquila, the Eagle, and its brightest star, Altair. The Summer Triangle is now complete, with Altair, Vega, and Deneb, the three brightest stars in the east, spanning a large portion of sky. In Lyra, adjacent to Vega, is Epsilon Lyrae, the well-known "double-double" star whose two components are each close double stars visible with 2-inch telescopes.

Looking toward the northern sky during early June evenings, the Big Dipper begins its descent in the northwest. The arcing handle points across the dome of the sky to Arcturus and farther down to Spica. Draco, the Dragon, its head lying north of Hercules, curls around the elevated part of the Little Dipper, Ursa Minor. Polaris stands in its usual place, at an altitude above the northern horizon that closely matches your latitude on Earth. Above Polaris, third- and fourth-magnitude stars mark the body of the Little Bear, and a faint line of fifth-magnitude stars trace down to Polaris. To the northeast of Polaris, Cepheus is beginning to rise with each hour. Below it, hugging the horizon, is Cassiopeia.

The Rho Ophiuchi region is located 700 light years away, filled with glowing gas and dark dust. Antares is the star to the lower left and to its right is the globular cluster M4. The blue reflection nebula is caused by starlight scattering off small dust particles.

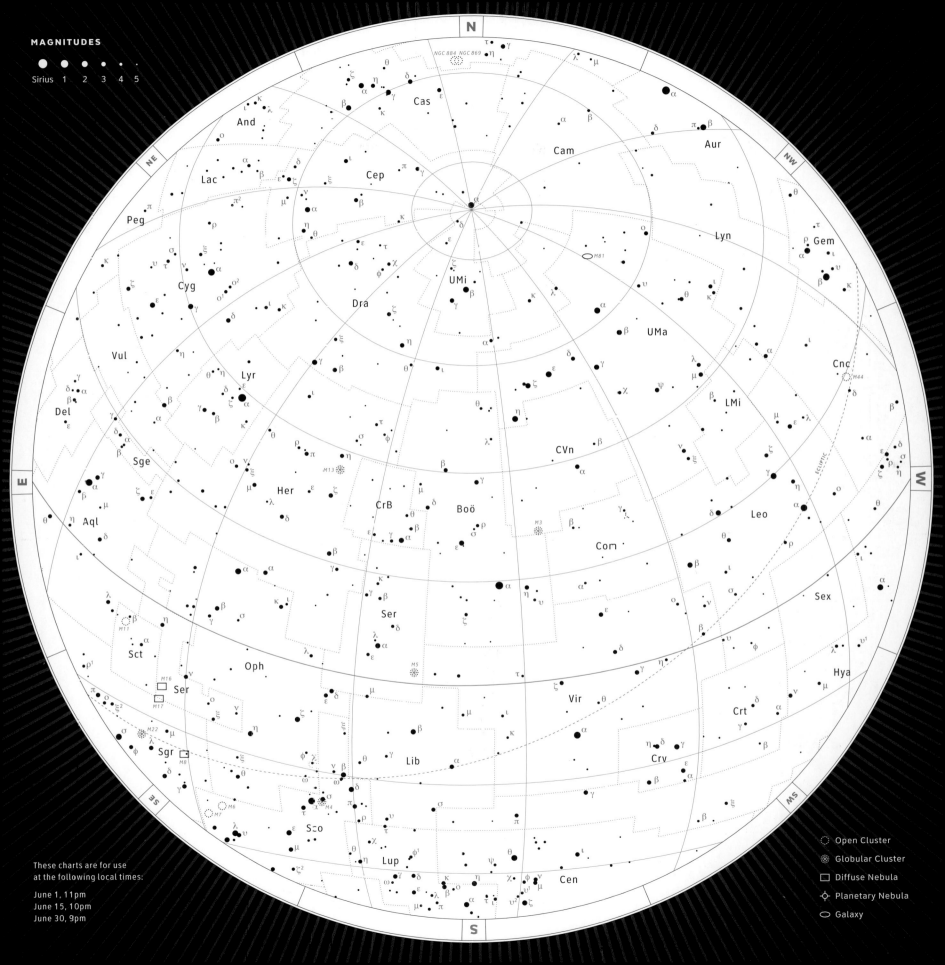

June

LIST OF CONSTELLATIONS

NAME	MEANING	ABBREV.
Aquila	Eagle	Aql
Auriga	Charioteer	Aur
Boötes	Herdsman	Boö
Camelopardalis	Giraffe	Cam
Cancer	Crab	Cnc
Canes Venatici	Hunting Dogs	CVn
Capricornus	Sea Goat	Cap
Cassiopeia	Queen	Cas
Cepheus	King	Cep
Centaurus	Centaur	Cen
Coma Berenices	Berenice's Hair	Com
Corona Borealis	North. Crown	CrB
Corvus	Crow	Crv
Cygnus	Swan	Cyg
Delphinus	Dolphin	Del
Draco	Dragon	Dra
Equuleus	Foal	Equ
Gemini	Twins	Gem
Hercules	Hercules	Her
Hydra	Water Snake	Hya
Lacerta	Lizard	Lac
Leo	Lion	Leo
Leo Minor	Lion Cub	LMi
Libra	Scales	Lib
Lupus	Wolf	Lup
Lynx	Lynx	Lyn
Lyra	Harp	Lyr
Ophiuchus	Serpent Bearer	Oph
Pegasus	Winged Horse	Peg
Sagitta	Arrow	Sge
Sagittarius	Archer	Sgr
Scorpius	Scorpion	Sco
Scutum	Shield	Sct
Serpens	Serpent	Ser
Sextans	Sextant	Sex
Ursa Minor	Little Bear	UMi
Ursa Major	Great Bear	UMa
Virgo	Virgin	Vir
Vulpecula	Fox	Vul

DEEP-SKY OBJECTS

These are the brightest of the deep-sky objects greater than magnitude 7 visible on this month's chart and are listed to the nearest whole magnitude. The visibility of deep-sky objects depends on their angular size. Galaxies and nebulae are extended objects and at magnitude 6 may still be difficult to make out because of low surface brightness.

OBJECT	LOCATION	TYPE	MAG.	COMMENTS
M3	Boötes	Globular Cluster	6	A bright globular cluster located between Arcturus and Cor Caroli, an excellent telescopic object.
M4	Scorpius	Globular Cluster	6	A fine globular cluster near the bright star Antares.
M5	Serpens	Globular Cluster	6	A bright globular cluster in a sparse region of sky, an excellent telescopic object.
M13	Hercules	Globular Cluster	5	The brightest northern hemisphere globular, visible in binoculars and best through telescopes.
M48	Hydra	Open Cluster	6	A good open cluster containing about 50 stars visible in binoculars.
M81	Ursa Major	Galaxy	7	Spiral galaxy visible in telescopes at low magnification, with a fainter edge-on neighboring galaxy, M82, lying within one degree.
γ Leonis	Leo	Double Star	2	Also called Algieba, a lovely telescopic, orange-yellow double star with a close third-magnitude companion.
α CVn	Canes Venatici	Double Star	3	Also called Cor Caroli, a fine telescopic double star with a fifth-magnitude companion.
Porrima	Virgo	Double Star	3	A fine pair of stars of equal brightness and color, easily split in small telescopes.
Izar	Boötes	Double star	2	One of the finest telescopic double stars in the sky consists of a pair of orange and blue stars.
ε Lyrae	Lyra	Double star	5	The famous "double-double" star. Two stars can be seen with the naked eye, and each component is double when viewed telescopically.

THE GREEK ALPHABET

LETTER	NAME	LETTER	NAME
α	alpha	ν	nu
β	beta	ξ	xi
γ	gamma	ο	omicron
δ	delta	π	pi
ε	epsilon	ρ	rho
ζ	zeta	σ	sigma
η	eta	τ	tau
θ	theta	υ	upsilon
ι	iota	φ	phi
κ	kappa	χ	chi
λ	lambda	ψ	psi
μ	mu	ω	omega

BRIGHTEST STARS

NAME	DESIG.	MAG.	DISTANCE (LY)
Arcturus	α Boö	0.0	37
Vega	α Lyr	0.0	25
Capella	α Aur	0.1	42
Altair	α Aql	0.8	17
Antares	α Sco	1.0	604
Spica	α Vir	1.0	262
Pollux	β Gem	1.1	34
Deneb	α Cyg	1.3	3,228
Regulus	α Leo	1.4	78
Shaula	λ Sco	1.6	703
Alioth	ε UMa	1.8	81
Dubhe	α UMa	1.8	124

July

The Milky Way rises in the eastern sky during July, but unfortunately many city dwellers will never see this magnificent feature of the night sky. The summer is the best time to see these neighboring stars of our own galaxy, so a trip to the country on a dark moonless night is well worth the effort.

Leo, the Lion, and its brightest star, Regulus, are about to exit the evening sky to the west. Virgo follows close behind, setting two hours later.

The Big Dipper is located high in the northwestern sky. The pointers, Dubhe and Merak, point to Polaris along a horizontal line, compared to a vertical line in April when the Dipper was overhead. Follow the arcing handle of the Dipper to find the bright orange star, Arcturus, high in the west-southwest. It's the brightest star in Boötes, the Herdsman, a kite-shaped group containing Izar, a beautiful telescopic double star.

The Eagle Nebula, M16, in Serpens, is a cluster of loosely scattered stars embedded in a cocoon of dust and gas. Subtle, faint glows of gas are visible in small telescopes.

The expansive constellation of Hercules, containing the globular cluster M13, passes virtually overhead. Larger telescopes will reveal many stars in this cluster. Corona Borealis, the Northern Crown, is a compact, curved line of stars nestled between Boötes and Hercules.

Serpens, the Serpent, is a long constellation split into two parts. One part lies southwest of Hercules. Ophiuchus, the Serpent-Bearer, lies between the two sections. The head, Serpens Caput, is the westernmost section. Serpens Cauda, the tail, lies to the east of Ophiuchus. Serpens Caput contains the bright globular cluster M5 while Serpens Cauda houses the beautiful Eagle Nebula M16.

Scorpius, a fine constellation that resembles the shape of a scorpion, is a long chain of bright stars headed by the bright star Antares.

Due west of Scorpius is Libra, the Scales. South of both constellations, lurking near the horizon, is Lupus, the Wolf. It's very low and is only visible from locations with an almost flat southern horizon.

The sky between Sagittarius, the Archer, and Scorpius is the direction of the center of our Milky Way galaxy. Observers lucky enough to view this region on a moonless night away from light pollution can see the central bulge of our galaxy. Sagittarius is full of deep-sky objects. Clouds of gas and dust, such as the Lagoon Nebula (M8) and the Omega Nebula (M17), are easily visible with binoculars.

The Summer Triangle dominates the eastern sky. Three bright stars in three constellations form this large triangle. The three stars are Altair, in Aquila, the Eagle; Deneb, in Cygnus, the Swan; and Vega, in Lyra, the Harp. The Milky Way runs through this region, and scanning it with a pair of binoculars is always a treat. For example,

The Lagoon Nebula, M8, in Sagittarius, is a glowing cloud of hydrogen gas visible in binoculars. Above M8 lies M20, the Trifid Nebula, a lovely combination of pink emission nebulosity, blue reflection nebulosity, and dark fingers of obscuring dust.

following the Milky Way through Aquila leads you into Scutum. Here you'll find M11, the "Wild Duck" open star cluster.

Rising in the east-northeast, setting the stage for fall, is the Square of Pegasus. Lacerta, Cepheus, and Cassiopeia are also rising in the northeast. As summer continues, the sky is already indicating the forthcoming change of seasons.

The Wild Duck open cluster, M11, lies over 5,000 light years from earth and contains nearly 700 stars; about 300 are visible in medium-sized telescopes. The cluster, found in Scutum, is about 20 light years across.

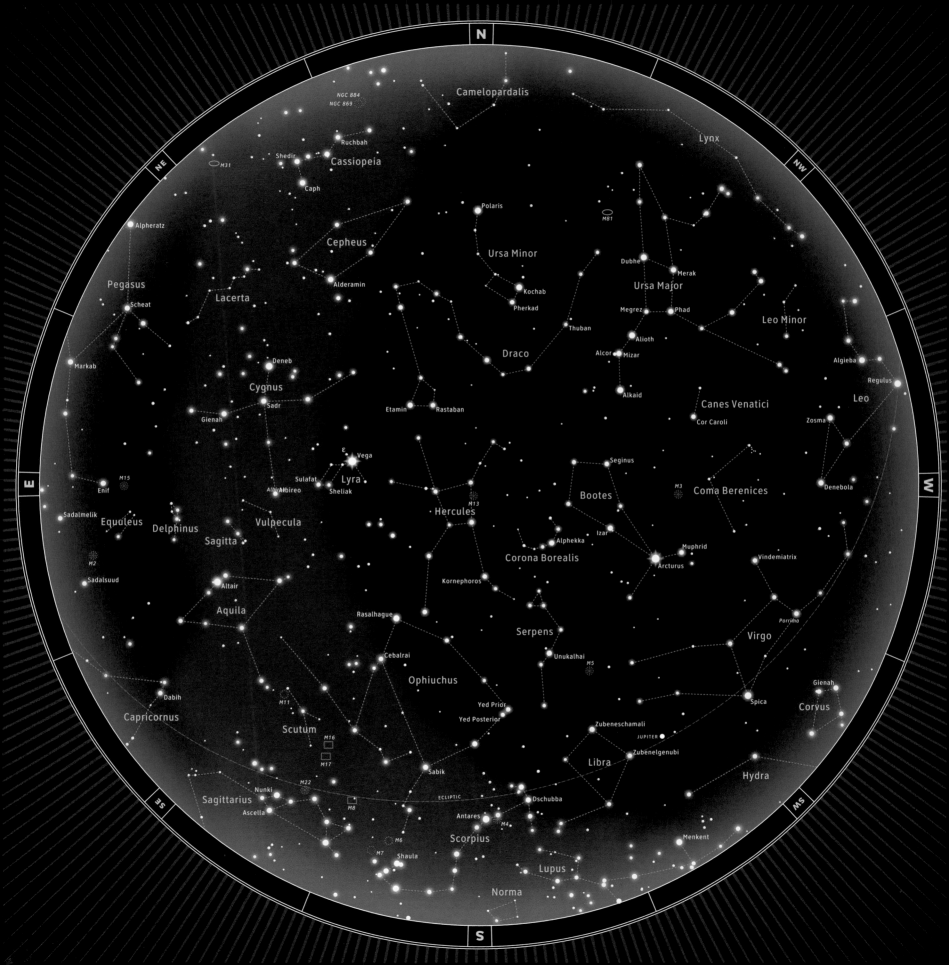

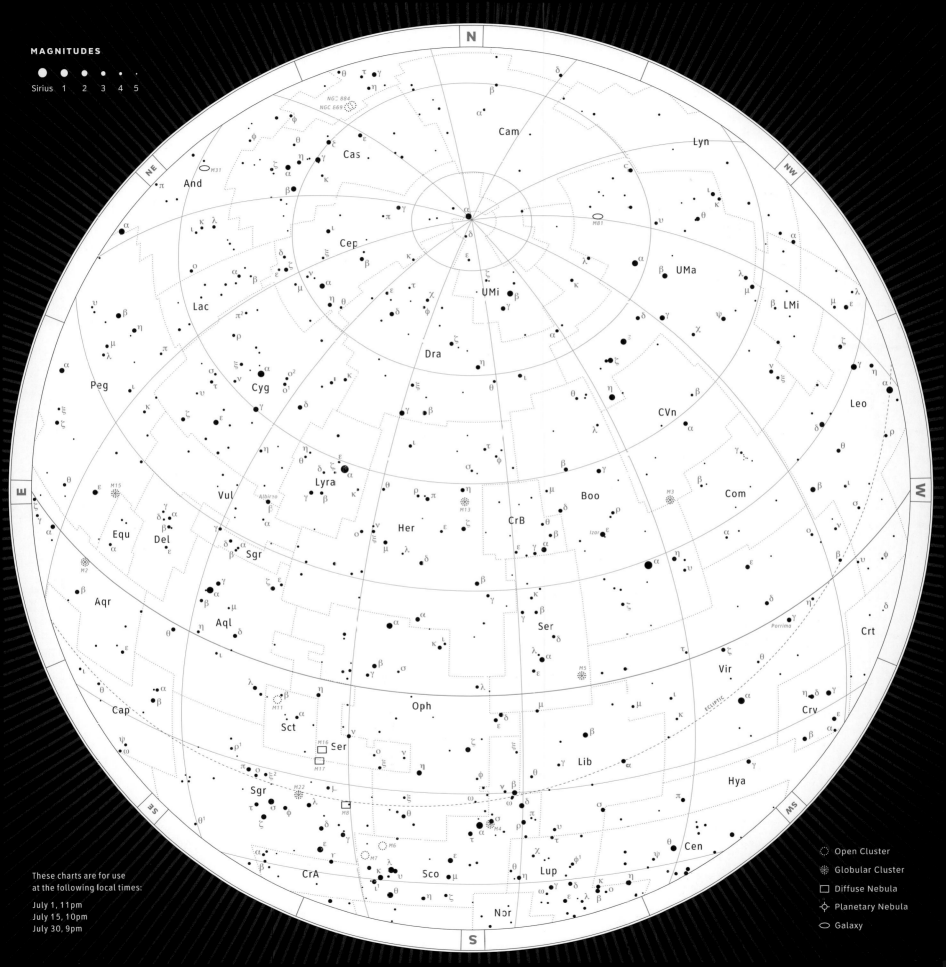

July

LIST OF CONSTELLATIONS

NAME	MEANING	ABBREV.
Aquila	Eagle	Aql
Boötes	Herdsman	Boö
Camelopardalis	Giraffe	Cam
Canes Venatici	Hunting Dogs	CVn
Capricornus	Sea Goat	Cap
Cassiopeia	Queen	Cas
Cepheus	King	Cep
Centaurus	Centaur	Cen
Coma Berenices	Berenice's Hair	Com
Corona Borealis	North. Crown	CrB
Corvus	Crow	Crv
Cygnus	Swan	Cyg
Delphinus	Dolphin	Del
Draco	Dragon	Dra
Equuleus	Foal	Equ
Hercules	Hercules	Her
Hydra	Water Snake	Hya
Lacerta	Lizard	Lac
Leo	Lion	Leo
Leo Minor	Lion Cub	LMi
Libra	Scales	Lib
Lupus	Wolf	Lup
Lynx	Lynx	Lyn
Lyra	Harp	Lyr
Norma	Rule	Nor
Ophiuchus	Serpent Bearer	Oph
Pegasus	Winged Horse	Peg
Sagitta	Arrow	Sge
Sagittarius	Archer	Sgr
Scorpius	Scorpion	Sco
Scutum	Shield	Sct
Serpens	Serpent	Ser
Ursa Minor	Little Bear	UMi
Ursa Major	Great Bear	UMa
Virgo	Virgin	Vir
Vulpecula	Fox	Vul

DEEP-SKY OBJECTS

These are the brightest of the deep-sky objects greater than magnitude 7 visible on this month's chart and are listed to the nearest whole magnitude. The visibility of deep-sky objects depends on their angular size. Galaxies and nebulae are extended objects and at magnitude 6 may still be difficult to make out because of low surface brightness.

OBJECT	LOCATION	TYPE	MAG.	COMMENTS
M3	Boötes	Globular Cluster	6	A bright globular cluster located between Arcturus and Cor Caroli, an excellent telescopic object.
M5	Serpens	Globular Cluster	6	A bright globular cluster in a sparse region of sky, an excellent telescopic object.
M6	Scorpius	Open Cluster	5	A loose, open cluster, 30 stars visible in binoculars.
M7	Scorpius	Open Cluster	3	A loose, open cluster, over 60 stars visible in binoculars.
M8	Sagittarius	Nebula	6	The Lagoon Nebula, a misty cloud, surrounds an embedded star cluster, an easy binocular object.
M11	Scutum	Open Cluster	6	The Wild Duck star cluster, an easy binocular object and lovely through a telescope.
M13	Hercules	Globular Cluster	5	The brightest northern hemisphere globular, visible in binoculars and best through a telescope.
M16	Serpens	Nebula	6	A star cluster embedded in faint nebula called the Eagle Nebula.
M17	Sagittarius	Nebula	6	Faint milky-white cloud visible in binoculars, called the Omega Nebula.
M22	Sagittarius	Globular Cluster	6	First globular discovered, a good telescopic object.
M81	Ursa Major	Galaxy	7	Spiral galaxy visible in telescopes at low magnification, with a fainter edge-on neighboring galaxy, M82, lying within one degree.
Izar	Boötes	Double star	2	One of the finest telescopic double stars in the sky consists of a pair of orange and blue stars.
ε Lyrae	Lyra	Double star	5	The famous "double-double" star. Two stars can be seen with the naked eye, and each component is double when viewed telescopically.

THE GREEK ALPHABET

LETTER	NAME	LETTER	NAME
α	alpha	ν	nu
β	beta	ξ	xi
γ	gamma	ο	omicron
δ	delta	π	pi
ε	epsilon	ρ	rho
ζ	zeta	σ	sigma
η	eta	τ	tau
θ	theta	υ	upsilon
ι	iota	φ	phi
κ	kappa	χ	chi
λ	lambda	ψ	psi
μ	mu	ω	omega

BRIGHTEST STARS

NAME	DESIG.	MAG.	DISTANCE (LY)
Arcturus	α Boö	0.0	37
Vega	α Lyr	0.0	25
Altair	α Aql	0.8	17
Antares	α Sco	1.0	604
Spica	α Vir	1.0	262
Deneb	α Cyg	1.3	3,228
Regulus	α Leo	1.4	78
Shaula	λ Sco	1.6	703
Alioth	ε UMa	1.8	81
Dubhe	α UMa	1.8	124
Kaus Austr.	ε Sgr	1.9	145
Alkaid	η UMa	1.9	101

August

Look high overhead in August and the brightest star you'll see is Vega, a brilliant, zero-magnitude star in the constellation of Lyra, the Harp. Lyra is one of the smallest constellations in the sky. Adjacent to Lyra is an easy binocular double star, Epsilon Lyrae, yet with a telescope each of these stars is, itself, double. This is the famous double-double star of Lyra.

Cygnus is part of the trio whose bright stars form the Summer Triangle. Cygnus hosts Deneb, a bright star even though it lies over 3,000 light years away. By comparison, Vega is only 25 light years away. The conclusion is that Deneb is a supergiant star.

At the southern end of Cygnus, the second-magnitude star Albireo is a telescopic treat.

It's a double star sporting a beautiful color contrast. One star appears yellow while the companion is bluish purple.

Follow the Milky Way through Cygnus to the south to find the bright star Altair flanked by two dimmer stars of similar brightness. The constellation is Aquila, the Eagle. Altair is only 16.8 light years from Earth.

Albireo, or Beta Cygni, is one of the finest double stars in the sky, and is visible with small telescopes. Their contrasting colors give away their surface temperature difference—the blue star is hotter than the yellow.

A line of stars to the south of Altair marks the head of the flying Eagle. This line extends into the constellation of Scutum. The Milky Way is rich with stars here, including M11, the Wild Duck open star cluster.

Sagittarius, the Archer, lies due south. The teapot-shaped group is rich with clusters, nebulae, and a myriad of faint stars in the distant Milky Way. The entire constellation of Scorpius lies in prone position in the south-southwest. The brilliant line of stars is also filled with star clusters worthy of a scan by binoculars or low-power telescope.

Above Scorpius, the large constellation of Ophiuchus creates a space relatively devoid of stars. There are numerous double stars and globular clusters in this region of space.

Five major constellations are entering the dome of the sky in its eastern half. Starting in the southeast, we find the faint group Capricornus, the Sea Goat. If your sky is hazy, or polluted by excessive light, most of the stars in this group will not be visible. Continuing a watery theme, Aquarius, the Water Bearer, rises next to Capricornus.

Moving north along the eastern horizon, Pisces, the Fish, is beginning to rise. The Square of Pegasus is already well up in the eastern sky. To the northeast, Andromeda, Perseus, and Cassiopeia are brightening the sky.

The Big Dipper is gliding slowly towards the northern horizon in its perpetual circling of the pole star in the northwestern sky. High above the Dipper, almost overhead, we find the small head of Draco, the Dragon. Its faint line

M17, in Sagittarius, is variously known as the Omega Nebula, the Swan Nebula, the Horseshoe Nebula, and the Lobster Nebula. It is an active "nursery" where stars are being formed in clouds of hydrogen gas.

M7 in Scorpius is a bright, loose open cluster of stars about 780 light years away, shown here with the backdrop of the more distant stars of the Milky Way.

of stars curves around Ursa Minor, ending just north of Dubhe, in the Big Dipper.

The western sky shows off the constellations of springtime, now far past their peak. Arcturus is lower in the west as each hour passes. Corona Borealis and Hercules follow. Virgo exits the sky soon after sunset, followed, in the southwest, by Libra.

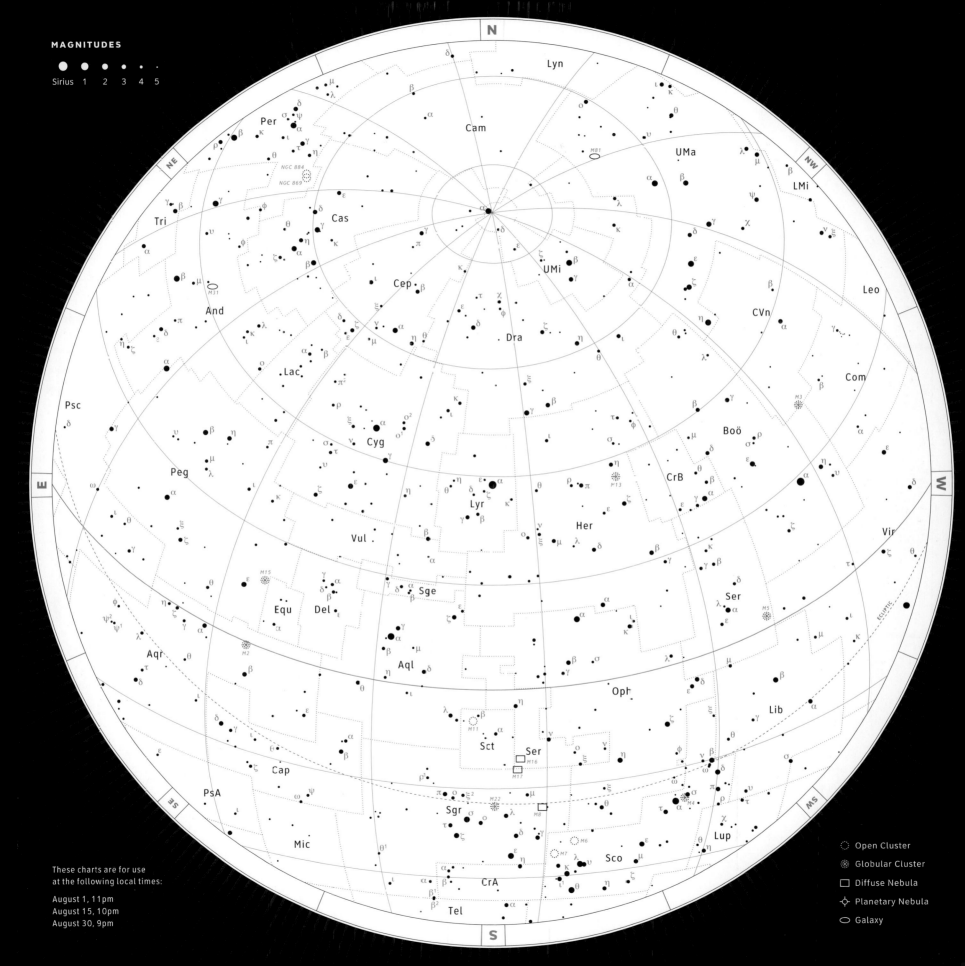

MAGNITUDES

Sirius 1 2 3 4 5

N

NE

NW

Lyn

Cam

UMa

Per

NGC 884

NGC 869

Tri

Cas

LMi

Cep

UMi

Leo

M31

And

Dra

CVn

Lac

Com

Psc

Cyg

Boö

M3

Peg

CrB

M13

E W

Lyr

Her

Vul

Ser

Vir

M15

Sge

M5

Equ

Del

Ser

Aqr

M2

Aql

Oph

Lib

Sct

Ser
M16

M17

Cap

M11

M22

M8

SE

PsA

Sgr

M4

MS

Mic

M6

Lup

M7

Sco

CrA

Tel

S

These charts are for use
at the following local times:

August 1, 11pm
August 15, 10pm
August 30, 9pm

◌ Open Cluster

⁛ Globular Cluster

□ Diffuse Nebula

◇ Planetary Nebula

◯ Galaxy

August

LIST OF CONSTELLATIONS

NAME	MEANING	ABBREV.
Andromeda	Princess	And
Aquarius	Water-Bearer	Aqr
Aquila	Eagle	Aql
Boötes	Herdsman	Boö
Camelopardalis	Giraffe	Cam
Canes Venatici	Hunting Dogs	CVn
Capricornus	Sea Goat	Cap
Cassiopeia	Queen	Cas
Cepheus	King	Cep
Centaurus	Centaur	Cen
Coma Berenices	Berenice's Hair	Com
Corona Australis	Southern Crown	CrA
Corona Borealis	Northern Crown	CrB
Cygnus	Swan	Cyg
Delphinus	Dolphin	Del
Draco	Dragon	Dra
Equuleus	Foal	Equ
Hercules	Hercules	Her
Lacerta	Lizard	Lac
Libra	Scales	Lib
Lyra	Harp	Lyr
Microscopium	Microscope	Mic
Ophiuchus	Serpent Bearer	Oph
Pegasus	Winged Horse	Peg
Perseus	Hero	Per
Pisces	Fish	Psc
Sagitta	Arrow	Sge
Sagittarius	Archer	Sgr
Scorpius	Scorpion	Sco
Scutum	Shield	Sct
Serpens	Serpent	Ser
Triangulum	Triangle	Tri
Ursa Minor	Little Bear	UMi
Ursa Major	Great Bear	UMa
Virgo	Virgin	Vir
Vulpecula	Fox	Vul

DEEP-SKY OBJECTS

These are the brightest of the deep-sky objects greater than magnitude 7 visible on this month's chart and are listed to the nearest whole magnitude. The visibility of deep-sky objects depends on their angular size. Galaxies and nebulae are extended objects and at magnitude 6 may still be difficult to make out because of low surface brightness.

OBJECT	LOCATION	TYPE	MAG.	COMMENTS
M2	Aquarius	Globular Cluster	6	Globular cluster with 100,000 stars packed into a space 40,000 light years across, fine telescopic object.
M5	Serpens	Globular Cluster	6	A bright globular cluster in a sparse region of sky, an excellent telescopic object.
M6	Scorpius	Open Cluster	5	A loose, open cluster, 30 stars visible in binoculars.
M7	Scorpius	Open Cluster	3	A loose, open cluster, over 60 stars visible in binoculars.
M8	Sagittarius	Nebula	6	The Lagoon Nebula, a misty cloud, surrounds an embedded star cluster, an easy binocular object.
M11	Scutum	Open Cluster	6	The Wild Duck star cluster, an easy binocular object and lovely through a telescope.
M13	Hercules	Globular Cluster	5	The brightest northern hemisphere globular, visible in binoculars and best through a telescope.
M16	Serpens	Nebula	6	A star cluster embedded in faint nebula called the Eagle Nebula.
M17	Sagittarius	Nebula	6	Faint, misty nebula visible in binoculars, called the Omega Nebula.
M22	Sagittarius	Globular Cluster	6	First globular discovered, a good telescopic object.
Izar	Boötes	Double star	2	One of the finest telescopic double stars in the sky consists of a pair of orange and blue stars.
ε Lyrae	Lyra	Double star	5	The famous "double-double" star. Two stars can be seen with the naked eye, and each component is double when viewed telescopically.
Albireo	Cygnus	Double star	3	A beautiful bluish-purple and yellow double star, excellent color contrast, best viewed through telescopes.

THE GREEK ALPHABET

LETTER	NAME	LETTER	NAME
α	alpha	ν	nu
β	beta	ξ	xi
γ	gamma	o	omicron
δ	delta	π	pi
ε	epsilon	ρ	rho
ζ	zeta	σ	sigma
η	eta	τ	tau
θ	theta	υ	upsilon
ι	iota	φ	phi
κ	kappa	χ	chi
λ	lambda	ψ	psi
μ	mu	ω	omega

BRIGHTEST STARS

NAME	DESIG.	MAG.	DISTANCE (LY)
Arcturus	α Boö	0.0	37
Vega	α Lyr	0.0	25
Altair	α Aql	0.8	17
Antares	α Sco	1.0	604
Spica	α Vir	1.0	262
Deneb	α Cyg	1.3	3,228
Shaula	λ Sco	1.6	703
Alioth	ε UMa	1.8	81
Mirfak	α Per	1.8	592
Dubhe	α UMa	1.8	124
Kaus Austr.	ε Sgr	1.9	145
Alkaid	η UMa	1.9	101

September

The September sky is one of transition. The season is changing from summer to fall and the fall equinox occurs after the third week of the month. The sun sets earlier each evening, providing an average of eight hours of nighttime before morning twilight brightens the sky for the next day.

The starry sky is also in transition. The brilliant stars of the Summer Triangle, Deneb, Vega, and Altair, start out high overhead in late evening as shown on this month's sky chart, and

The spectacular globular cluster M13 in Hercules contains hundreds of thousands or perhaps even millions of stars.

begin their slow descent toward the western or northwestern horizon during the night. The Milky Way runs north-south through Cygnus, Aquila, Scutum, and Sagittarius in the early evening and slowly turns with these stars to align in an east-west aspect shortly after midnight.

Arcturus is setting in the west, followed gracefully by the Northern Crown (Corona Borealis) and Hercules. Between Hercules and Sagittarius is the sprawling constellation of Ophiuchus. You can find several globular clusters in this constellation alone.

Low in the southwestern sky, the brightest part of the Milky Way in Sagittarius is

descending from view. The cooler and earlier evenings provide excellent opportunities for viewing this most stunning part of the Milky Way. The center of our galaxy sits in this direction, where the Milky Way is at its broadest, and represents the galaxy's central bulge. It's well worth venturing out to the country for a dark southwestern sky to fully enjoy this September treat.

To the east of Sagittarius lies the faint constellation of Capricornus, now standing at its highest in the sky to the south.

Rising in the eastern sky is the comparatively faint group of constellations of Aquarius, Pegasus, Pisces, and Cetus. But don't let their faintness trick you into thinking this part of the sky is dull. There are many deep-sky objects hidden here, some bright enough to be visible in binoculars, including M2, M15, and Mira.

Low in the southeast is the southernmost first-magnitude star, Fomalhaut, part of the constellation of Piscis Austrinus (the Southern Fish). It's easy to identify since a line joining the pair of stars on the right side of the square of Pegasus, and projected south, points straight to this well-known star.

Looking north and high above Polaris lies Cepheus. This faint group has the appearance of a child's drawing of a simple house, complete with an asymmetrical roof. Northeast of Cepheus is the five-star group of Cassiopeia. Appearing like an M or W depending on its orientation to the observer, Cassiopeia lies on its side in September and by midnight replaces Cygnus high overhead. Following Cassiopeia, and lower in the northeastern sky, is Perseus. Don't miss the famous

This image of the Andromeda Galaxy, M31, shows the dark lanes of dust similar to those seen in the photograph below of our own Milky Way galaxy.

This stunning image of our Milky Way galaxy reveals the dark rifts of dust and bright red glowing areas from clouds of hydrogen in its central area in Sagittarius.

double cluster of stars lying between these two constellations. The bright star low in the northeast is Capella; the brightest star in Auriga, the Charioteer.

The most familiar constellation of Ursa Major is sinking in the north-northwest. Its arcing handle points to the setting Arcturus, low in the northwest.

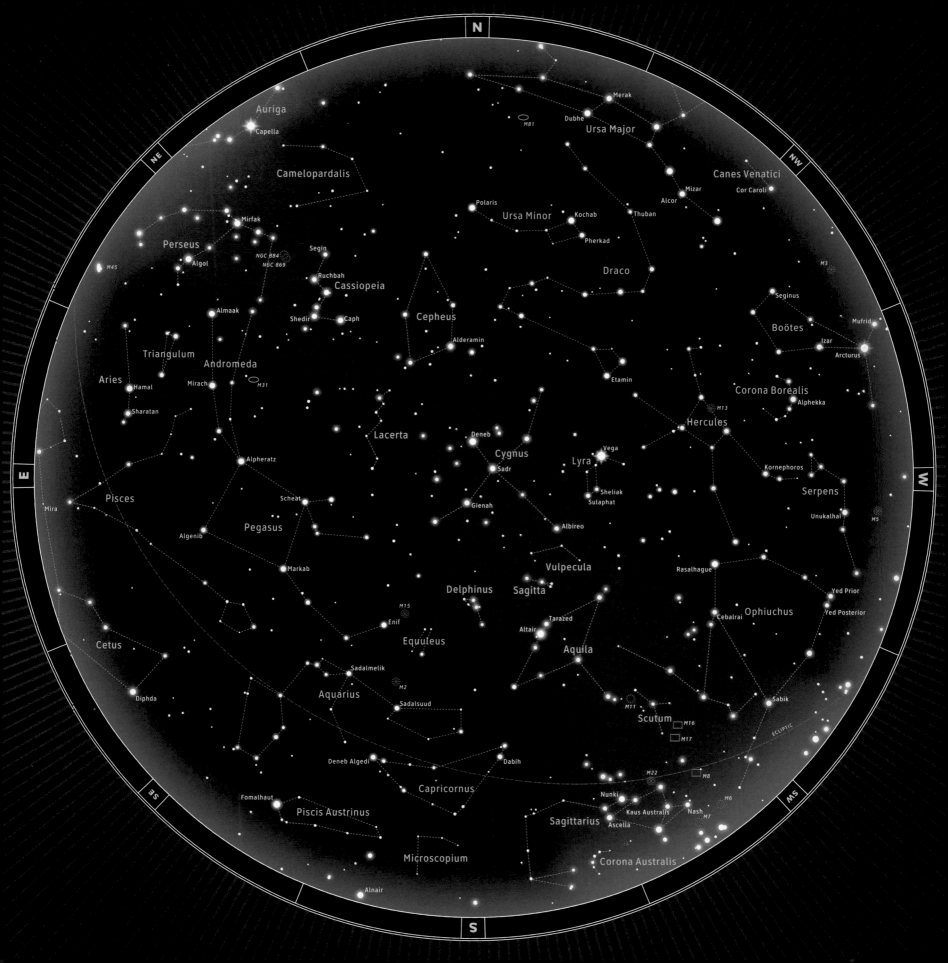

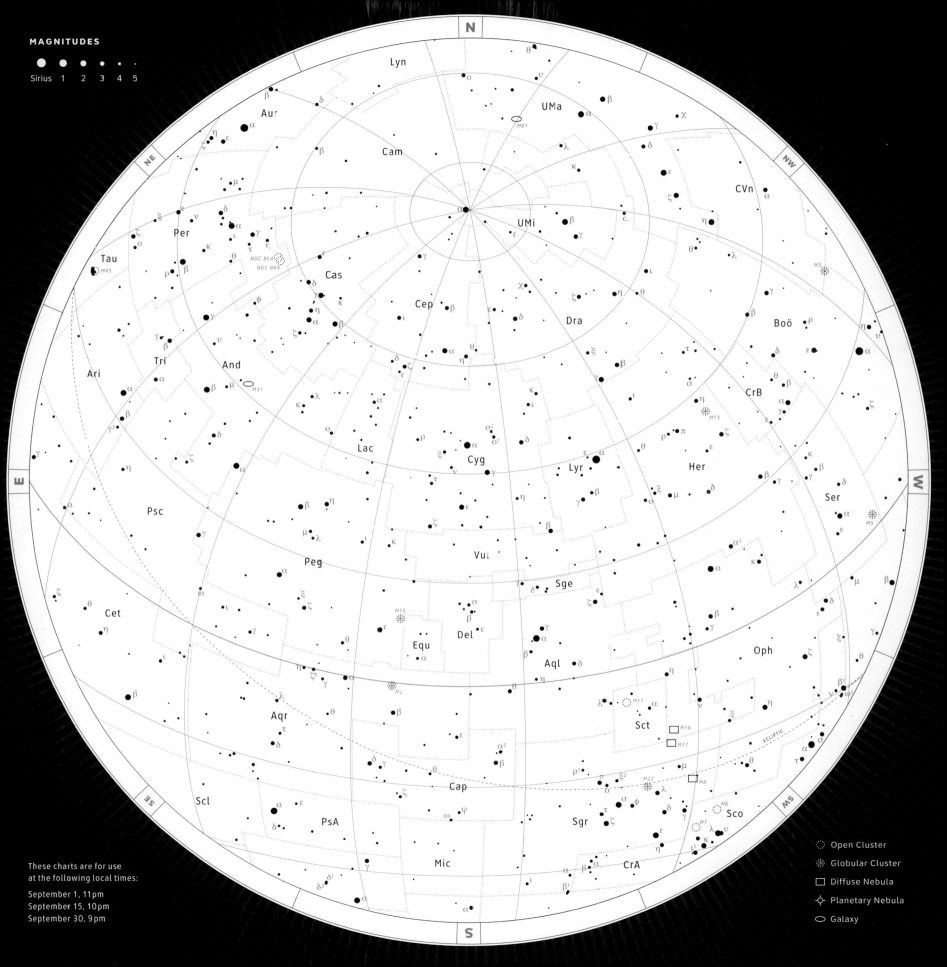

September

LIST OF CONSTELLATIONS

NAME	MEANING	ABBREV.
Andromeda	Princess	And
Aquarius	Water Bearer	Aqr
Aquila	Eagle	Aql
Aries	Ram	Ari
Auriga	Charioteer	Aur
Boötes	Herdsman	Boö
Camelopardalis	Giraffe	Cam
Canis Venatici	Hunting Dogs	Cvn
Capricornus	Sea Goat	Cap
Cassiopeia	Queen	Cas
Cepheus	King	Cep
Cetus	Whale	Cet
Corona Australis	Southern Crown	CrA
Corona Borealis	Northern Crown	CrB
Cygnus	Swan	Cyg
Delphinus	Dolphin	Del
Draco	Dragon	Dra
Equuleus	Foal	Equ
Hercules	Hercules	Her
Lacerta	Lizard	Lac
Lyncis	Lynx	Lyn
Lyra	Harp	Lyr
Microscopium	Microscope	Mic
Ophiuchus	Serpent Bearer	Oph
Pegasus	Winged Horse	Peg
Perseus	Hero	Per
Pisces	Fish	Psc
Pisces Austrinus	Southern Fish	PsA
Sagitta	Arrow	Sge
Sagittarius	Archer	Sgr
Scutum	Shield	Sct
Serpens	Serpent	Ser
Taurus	Bull	Tau
Triangulum	Triangle	Tri
Ursa Major	Great Bear	UMa
Ursa Minor	Little Bear	UMi
Vulpecula	Fox	Vul

DEEP-SKY OBJECTS

These are the brightest of the deep-sky objects greater than magnitude 7 visible on this month's chart and are listed to the nearest whole magnitude. The visibility of deep-sky objects depends on their angular size. Galaxies and nebulae are extended objects and at magnitude 6 may still be difficult to make out because of low surface brightness.

OBJECT	LOCATION	TYPE	MAG.	COMMENTS
M2	Aquarius	Globular Cluster	6	A fuzzy star in binoculars and best viewed with a telescope.
M10	Ophiuchus	Globular Cluster	7	A dim fuzzy star in binoculars and best viewed with a telescope.
M12	Ophiuchus	Globular Cluster	7	A dim fuzzy star in binoculars and best viewed with a telescope.
M13	Hercules	Globular Cluster	5	The best globular cluster in the northern sky, easily viewed with binoculars and best through a telescope.
M15	Pegasus	Globular Cluster	6	One of the brightest globular clusters in the autumn sky, faintly visible in binoculars as a fuzzy star and best through a telescope.
M30	Capricornus	Globular Cluster	7	Located in a sparsely populated region of sky, difficult to find.
M31	Andromeda	Galaxy	4	Binoculars show a faint, hazy, elongated cloud, best viewed with binoculars or low-power telescope.
M33	Triangulum	Galaxy	6	A difficult object to see due to low surface brightness—best viewed in binoculars—very faint.
NGC 869 & NGC 884	Perseus	Double Cluster/ Open Clusters	4	Two open clusters, best seen with binoculars.
Mira	Cetus	Variable Star	3–9	Famous variable star, sometimes visible to the naked eye but often requires binoculars.
Algol	Perseus	Variable Star	2–3	Every 2–3 days Algol drops by nearly a magnitude due to a fainter orbiting companion eclipsing the brighter object.
Albireo	Cygnus	Double Star	3	Telescopes show beautiful bluish-purple and yellow double star, excellent color contrast.
γ Andromedae	Andromeda	Double Star	2	An orange and blue star provide an excellent color contrast visible in small telescopes.

THE GREEK ALPHABET

LETTER	NAME	LETTER	NAME
α	alpha	ν	nu
β	beta	ξ	xi
γ	gamma	ο	omicron
δ	delta	π	pi
ε	epsilon	ρ	rho
ζ	zeta	σ	sigma
η	eta	τ	tau
θ	theta	υ	upsilon
ι	iota	φ	phi
κ	kappa	χ	chi
λ	lambda	ψ	psi
μ	mu	ω	omega

BRIGHTEST STARS

NAME	DESIG.	MAG	DISTANCE (LY)
Arcturus	α Boö	0.0	37
Vega	α Lyr	0.0	25
Capella	α Aur	0.1	42
Altair	α Aql	0.8	17
Antares	α Sco	1.0	604
Fomalhaut	α PsA	1.2	25
Deneb	α Cyg	1.3	3,228
Alioth	ε UMa	1.8	81
Mirfak	α Per	1.8	592
Dubhe	α UMa	1.8	124
Kaus Aust.	ε Sgr	1.9	145
Alkaid	η UMa	1.9	101

October

Fall foliage colors are well underway in many areas of the northern hemisphere and after sunset, occurring noticeably earlier than in previous weeks, the beautiful fall sky is on view. The summer stars are descending into the west and the winter stars are beginning to display their brilliant lights from the east.

Vega, the brightest star in Lyra, leads the Summer Triangle towards the western horizon. Altair lies high in the southwest, while Deneb, in Cygnus the Swan, remains at a high altitude in the west. Observers in locales with very little light pollution will see the two bands of Milky Way divided by a dark rift arcing through Cygnus. Following a summer where the Milky Way was aligned north-south, it has turned to run from the northeast to the southwest by the time of October's chart.

By tracing the band of the Milky Way high overhead, we find the dim group Lacerta the Lizard. Like its name-sake, this constellation creeps into place almost unnoticed. Cassiopeia is adjacent and lies in the north-east. Its familiar W-shape is lying on its side this month.

The southeastern sky is a very sparse region of stars. High above the horizon, the Square of Pegasus dominates with Pisces, the Fish, represented by a particularly faint line of stars located below it. Adjacent to the Square is Andromeda whose stars stretch out in the direction of Perseus, now high in the northeast. In the same direction as the stars in Andromeda is the much more distant Andromeda Galaxy, visible in binoculars as an elongated fuzzy cloud.

One of the circumpolar constellations, Cassiopeia is visible year-round. The five brightest stars form the familiar W-shape.

Below Pisces we find Cetus, the Whale. There are a couple of brighter stars in this constellation, now stretched out along the southeastern horizon. Its most famous star is Mira, the Wonderful. This star is variable and can, at times, shine at third magnitude.

The first-magnitude star, Fomalhaut, lies low in the south, aligned with the two stars down the right side of the Square of Pegasus. Fomalhaut is part of the faint group Piscis Austrinus. Low in the southwest we find Capricornus. Sagittarius disappears over the southwestern horizon as the twilight glow diminishes.

Now look to the east to see the first of the brilliant stars of winter rising. Taurus, with its attendant Pleiades star cluster (M45), appears first, followed by the V-shaped Hyades cluster and Aldebaran, the eye of the Bull.

The brilliant star Capella appears low in the northeast, a yellowish star joined by the attendant stars of Auriga, the Charioteer. Climbing higher still from the northwest is the misshapen K-shape of Perseus.

The Pole star remains where it is all year with the stars of Ursa Minor circling around it. Draco, the Dragon, slithers around the region of Ursa Minor to the northwest. Sitting on the northern horizon, Ursa Minor's larger sibling, the Great Bear, will be hidden by trees or houses for most observers.

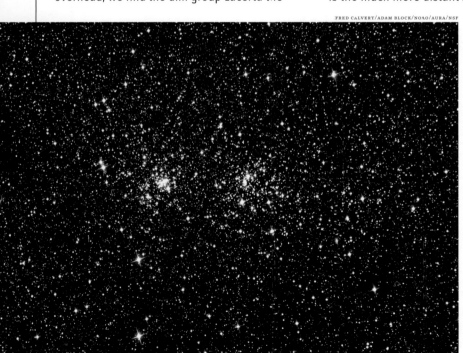

The Double Cluster in Perseus, NGC 869 and NGC 884, is a dazzling sprinkling of stars and makes for a wonderful sight in binoculars.

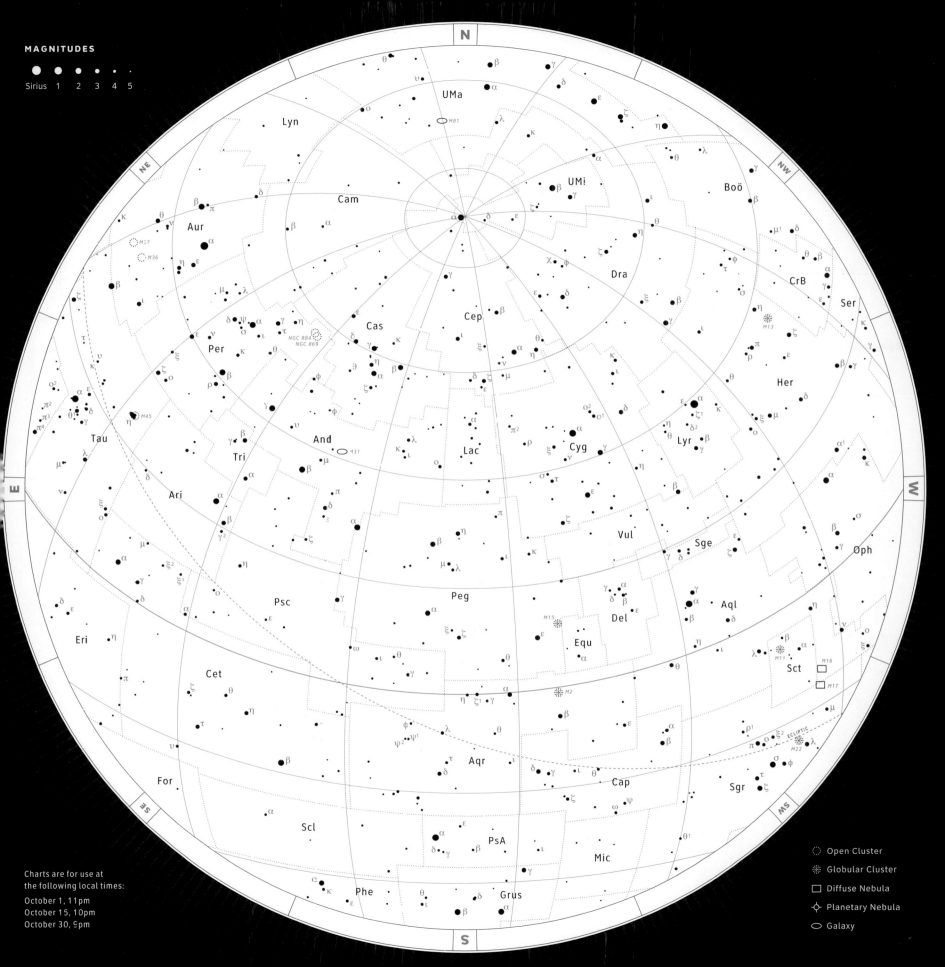

N

NE

NW

E

W

SE

SW

S

Lyn

UMa

M81

UMi

Boö

β

γ

δ

α

ν

ο

λ

κ

ζ

η

β

γ

Cam

Dra

CrB

Ser

Aur

κ

θ

ν

β

π

α

η

ε

μ

λ

β

ι

M37

M36

α

δ

β

α

γ

χ

φ

ζ

τ

θ

φ

α

μ¹

δ

θ

ι

ζ

η

M13

ζ

ρ

ε

γ

Per

Cas

Cep

Her

δ

ψ

α

γ

η

σ

ι

NGC 884
NGC 869

ξ

θ

ε

δ

ξ

μ

θ

δ

μ

ζ

ο

β

ϑ

η

α

κ

ξ

π²

ο²

ο¹

α

ε

ζ¹

κ

μ

ρ

φ

γ

υ

φ

δ²

σ

τ

And

Lac

Cyg

Lyr

M31

θ

γ

δ²

δ

ο²

π¹

π²

θ

α

ε

ζ

Tri

Psc

α

β

α¹

κ

Ari

Peg

Vul

Sge

Oph

γ²

β

η

β

η

γ

δ

β

α

Del

Aql

β

η

λ

α

σ

Eri

ε

δ

M15

Equ

M11

β

Sct
M16

M17

Cet

ω

M2

μ

φ

ψ²

ψ¹

λ

θ

ζ¹

γ

ρ¹

ξ

ECLIPTIC

λ

M22

β

For

Aqr

Cap

σ

φ

Sgr

τ

ζ

Scl

Phe

PsA

Mic

α

δ

γ

θ

δ

β

Grus

October

LIST OF CONSTELLATIONS

NAME	MEANING	ABBREV.
Andromeda	Princess	And
Aquarius	Water Bearer	Aqr
Aquila	Eagle	Aql
Aries	Ram	Ari
Auriga	Charioteer	Aur
Camelopardalis	Giraffe	Cam
Capricornus	Sea Goat	Cap
Cassiopeia	Queen	Cas
Cepheus	King	Cep
Cetus	Whale	Cet
Cygnus	Swan	Cyg
Delphinus	Dolphin	Del
Draco	Dragon	Dra
Eridanus	River	Eri
Equuleus	Foal	Equ
Fornax	Lab. Furnace	For
Hercules	Hercules	Her
Lacerta	Lizard	Lac
Lynx	Lynx	Lyn
Lyra	Harp	Lyr
Microscopium	Microscope	Mic
Pegasus	Winged Horse	Peg
Perseus	Hero	Per
Phoenix	Phoenix	Phe
Pisces	Fish	Psc
Piscis Austrinus	Southern Fish	PsA
Sagitta	Arrow	Sge
Sagittarius	Archer	Sgr
Sculptor	Sculpt. Wrkshp.	Scl
Scutum	Shield	Sct
Taurus	Bull	Tau
Triangulum	Triangle	Tri
Ursa Minor	Little Bear	UMi
Ursa Major	Great Bear	UMa

DEEP-SKY OBJECTS

These are the brightest of the deep-sky objects greater than magnitude 7 visible on this month's chart and are listed to the nearest whole magnitude. The visibility of deep-sky objects depends on their angular size. Galaxies and nebulae are extended objects and at magnitude 6 may still be difficult to make out because of low surface brightness.

OBJECT	LOCATION	TYPE	MAG.	COMMENTS
M2	Aquarius	Globular Cluster	6	*Globular cluster with 100,000 stars packed into a space 40,000 light years across, an excellent telescopic object.*
M15	Pegasus	Globular Cluster	6	*A compact globular cluster, best viewed through a telescope.*
NCG 869 & NGC 884	Perseus	Open Cluster	4	*The Double Cluster, two fine, rich, open clusters, best seen with binoculars.*
M31	Andromeda	Galaxy	4	*Andromeda Galaxy, a faint, hazy, elongated cloud, best viewed with binoculars or low-power telescope.*
M33	Triangulum	Galaxy	6	*An elusive object due to low surface brightness—best viewed in binoculars—very faint.*
M36	Auriga	Open Cluster	6	*M36 and M37 are visible as fuzzy spots through binoculars and beautiful open star clusters when viewed through a small telescope.*
M37	Auriga	Open Cluster	6	*See M36 notes.*
M45	Taurus	Open Cluster	2	*The Pleiades, also Seven Sisters, a naked eye object, excellent in binoculars, with nearly 100 stars visible in small telescopes.*
Mira	Cetus	Variable Star	3–9	*Famous variable star, sometimes naked eye, or faint enough to need binoculars to see it.*
Algol	Perseus	Variable Star	2–3	*Every 2–3 days Algol drops by nearly a magnitude due to a fainter orbiting companion eclipsing the brighter object.*
Albireo	Cygnus	Double star	3	*A beautiful bluish-purple and yellow double star, excellent color contrast, best viewed through telescopes.*
γ Andromedae	Andromeda	Double star	2	*An orange and blue star form an excellent color contrast best viewed through a telescope.*

THE GREEK ALPHABET

LETTER	NAME	LETTER	NAME
α	alpha	ν	nu
β	beta	ξ	xi
γ	gamma	ο	omicron
δ	delta	π	pi
ε	epsilon	ρ	rho
ζ	zeta	σ	sigma
η	eta	τ	tau
θ	theta	υ	upsilon
ι	iota	φ	phi
κ	kappa	χ	chi
λ	lambda	ψ	psi
μ	mu	ω	omega

BRIGHTEST STARS

NAME	DESIG.	MAG	DISTANCE (LY)
Vega	α Lyr	0.0	25
Capella	α Aur	0.1	42
Altair	α Aql	0.8	17
Aldebaran	α Tau	0.9	65
Fomalhaut	α PsA	1.2	25
Deneb	α Cyg	1.3	3,228
Alnath	β Tau	1.7	131
Alioth	ε UMa	1.8	81
Mirfak	α Per	1.8	592
Dubhe	α UMa	1.8	124
Alkaid	η UMa	1.9	101
Menkalinan	β Aur	1.9	82

November

Evening comes early during November, offering eleven hours of sky-watching opportunities. Two of the brilliant stars of the Summer Triangle descend toward the western horizon: Altair lies due west and Vega is in the northwest, the brightest star in November's early evening sky. Deneb, the Swan's brightest orb, will take longer to reach the horizon, standing high in the west. Look

to Enif—you'll find globular cluster M15 within the same binocular field of view as this star.

Low in the southwest, well below the right side of the Square of Pegasus, lies the first-magnitude star Fomalhaut, in Piscis Austrinus. Observers with a very clear southern horizon may glimpse two or three stars of the Phoenix.

Farther west the now-setting Capricornus is exiting the sky's stage, with Aquarius, the Water-Bearer, following it closely.

Two lesser-known constellations lie east of Piscis Austrinus. First is Sculptor, home to the southern pole of the Milky Way galaxy. You'll need a clear southern horizon to spot this group. South of Cetus, the Whale, lies an even fainter group, Fornax. Low in the southeast adjacent to Fornax is the winding line of stars making up the River, Eridanus.

Sitting on the eastern horizon, as if reclining before a full winter appearance, is Orion, the Hunter. Gazing to the northeast the

M15, in Pegasus, lies within the same binocular field of view as Epsilon Pegasi. This globular cluster lies 30,000 light years from Earth and is 160 light years across.

Found in Taurus, the Pleiades, M45, is the finest open cluster in the sky. Also known as the Seven Sisters, the cluster contains hundreds of hot, blue stars.

pair of stars called Castor and Pollux announce the rising of Gemini, the Twins who, like Orion, also appears in a state of repose.

By tracing the band of the Milky Way high overhead, we find Cassiopeia with its familiar W-shape (or M if you are facing north). Adjacent to Cassiopeia and high overhead is Andromeda whose stars stretch out from Pegasus to Perseus. In the same direction as the stars in Andromeda is the much more distant Andromeda Galaxy. The best time for viewing our neighboring spiral galaxy occurs during November when it passes high overhead.

The Big Dipper has completed its low swing under Polaris and is preparing to climb in the northeast, just as the head of Draco, the Dragon, is descending in the northwest. Cepheus stands high above Draco and both of these constellations are descending in the northwest.

how the Milky Way has completed its turn from north-south in summer to its east-west alignment in November.

The Square of Pegasus stands high and rules the southern aspect of the sky. Its four stars of second magnitude define the square with few other stars around it. Follow the line of three stars from the lower right corner

The sprawling constellation of Cetus, the Whale, and Pisces, the Fish, fill the sparse region southeast of Pegasus. Mira Ceti is a favorite long-period variable star with a 332-day period and can shine as bright as third magnitude or as dim as ninth magnitude. Cetus has a couple of brighter stars, while Pisces is a very faint group.

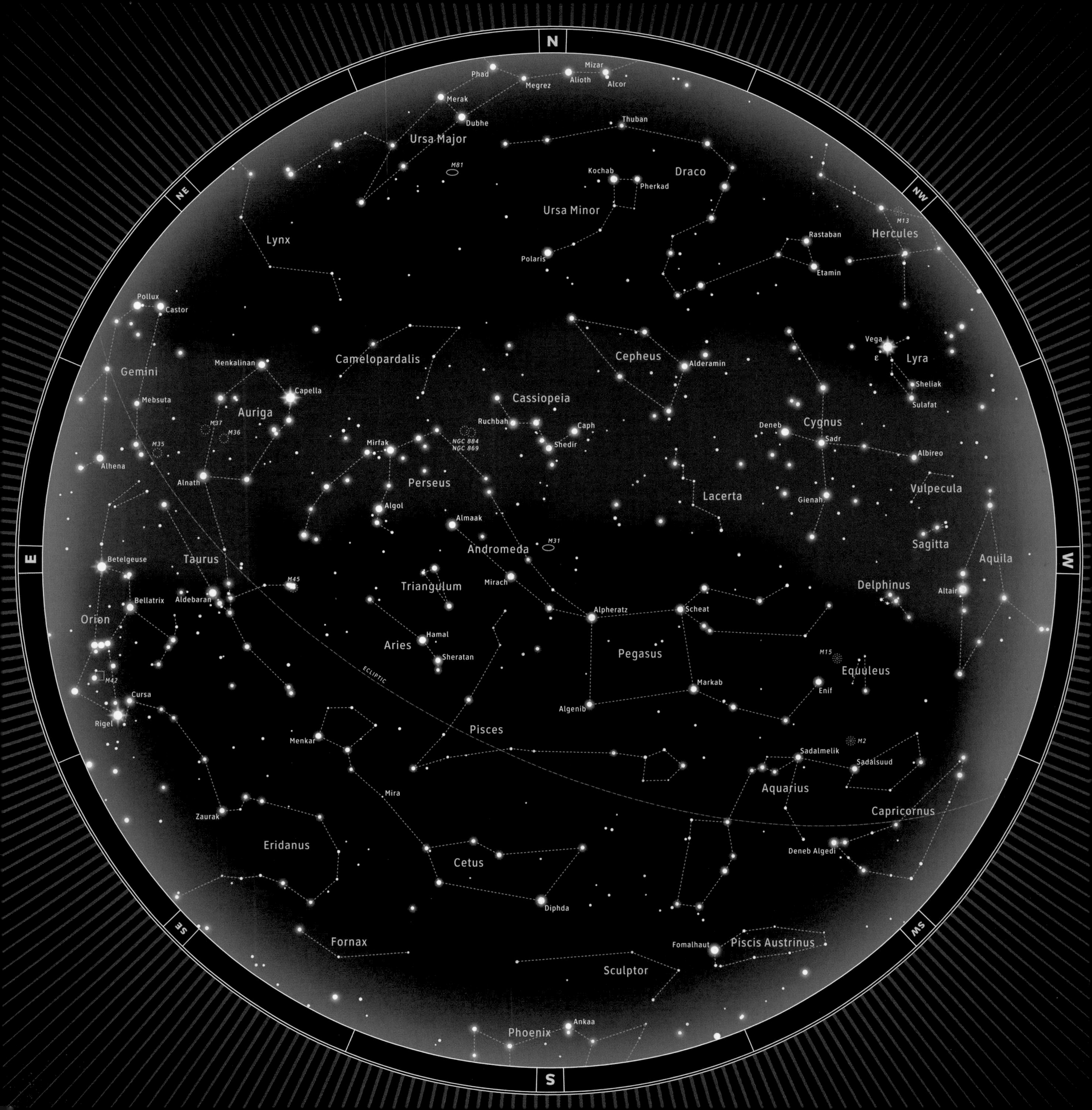

N
NE
E
SE
S
SW
W
NW
Phad
Megrez
Alioth
Mizar
Alcor
Merak
Dubhe
Ursa Major
M81
Thuban
Draco
Kochab
Pherkad
Ursa Minor
Polaris
Lynx
Rastaban
M13
Hercules
Etamin
Pollux
Castor
Gemini
Mebsuta
M35
Alhena
Menkalinan
Capella
Auriga
M37
M36
Alnath
Camelopardalis
Cepheus
Alderamin
Vega
ε
Lyra
Sheliak
Sulafat
Cassiopeia
Ruchbah
Caph
Shedir
NGC 884
NGC 869
Mirfak
Perseus
Algol
Deneb
Cygnus
Sadr
Albireo
Lacerta
Gienah
Vulpecula
Almaak
Andromeda
M31
Sagitta
Aquila
Betelgeuse
Taurus
M45
Triangulum
Mirach
Delphinus
Altair
Bellatrix
Aldebaran
Orion
Alpheratz
Scheat
Aries
Hamal
Sheratan
Pegasus
M15
Equuleus
M42
ECLIPTIC
Markab
Enif
Cursa
Rigel
Algenib
Pisces
Menkar
M2
Sadalmelik
Sadalsuud
Mira
Aquarius
Zaurak
Capricornus
Eridanus
Deneb Algedi
Cetus
Diphda
Fornax
Fomalhaut
Piscis Austrinus
Sculptor
Ankaa
Phoenix

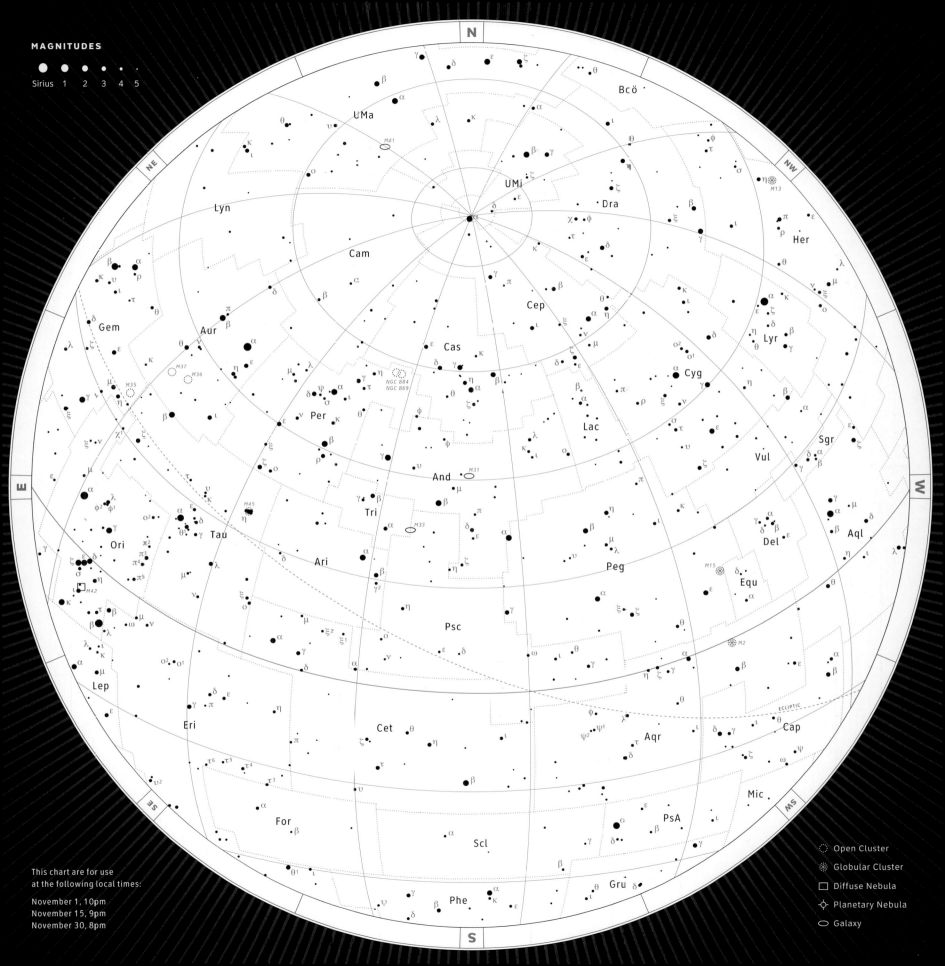

MAGNITUDES

Sirius 1 2 3 4 5

N

NE

NW

E

W

SE

MS

S

This chart are for use
at the following local times:

November 1, 10pm
November 15, 9pm
November 30, 8pm

Open Cluster
Globular Cluster
Diffuse Nebula
Planetary Nebula
Galaxy

November

LIST OF CONSTELLATIONS

NAME	MEANING	ABBREV.
Andromeda	Princess	And
Aquarius	Water Bearer	Aqr
Aquila	Eagle	Aql
Aries	Ram	Ari
Auriga	Charioteer	Aur
Camelopardalis	Giraffe	Cam
Capricornus	Sea Goat	Cap
Cassiopeia	Queen	Cas
Cepheus	King	Cep
Cetus	Whale	Cet
Cygnus	Swan	Cyg
Delphinus	Dolphin	Del
Draco	Dragon	Dra
Eridanus	River	Eri
Equuleus	Foal	Equ
Fornax	Lab. Furnace	For
Gemini	Twins	Gem
Hercules	Hercules	Her
Lacerta	Lizard	Lac
Lynx	Lynx	Lyn
Lyra	Harp	Lyr
Orion	Hunter	Ori
Pegasus	Winged Horse	Peg
Perseus	Hero	Per
Phoenix	Phoenix	Phe
Pisces	Fish	Psc
Piscis Austrinus	Southern Fish	PsA
Sagitta	Arrow	Sge
Sculptor	Sculpt. Wrkshp.	Scl
Taurus	Bull	Tau
Triangulum	Triangle	Tri
Ursa Minor	Little Bear	UMi
Ursa Major	Great Bear	UMa
Vulpecula	Fox	Vul

DEEP-SKY OBJECTS

These are the brightest of the deep-sky objects greater than magnitude 7 visible on this month's chart and are listed to the nearest whole magnitude. The visibility of deep-sky objects depends on their angular size. Galaxies and nebulae are extended objects and at magnitude 6 may still be difficult to make out because of low surface brightness.

OBJECT	LOCATION	TYPE	MAG.	COMMENTS
M2	Aquarius	Globular Cluster	6	Globular cluster with 100,000 stars packed into a space 40,000 light years across, an excellent telescopic object.
M15	Pegasus	Globular Cluster	6	One of the brightest globular clusters in the autumn sky, faintly visible in binoculars as a fuzzy star and best through a telescope.
NCG 869 & NGC 884	Perseus	Open Cluster	4	The Double Cluster, two fine, rich, open clusters, best seen with binoculars.
M31	Andromeda	Galaxy	4	Andromeda Galaxy, a faint, hazy, elongated cloud, best viewed with binoculars or low power telescope.
M33	Triangulum	Galaxy	6	An elusive object due to low surface brightness—best viewed in binoculars—very faint.
M36	Auriga	Open Cluster	6	M36 and M37 are visible as fuzzy spots through binoculars and beautiful open star clusters when viewed through a small telescope.
M37	Auriga	Open Cluster	6	See M36 notes.
M42	Orion	Nebula	5	The Orion Nebula, the finest star forming region on view, visible in binoculars as a fuzzy star, and spectacular in any telescope. The central four stars arranged in a trapezoid shape.
M45	Taurus	Open Cluster	2	The Pleiades, also Seven Sisters, a naked eye object, excellent in binoculars, with nearly 100 stars visible in small telescopes.
Mira	Cetus	Variable Star	3–9	Famous variable star, sometimes naked eye, or faint enough to need binoculars to see it.
Algol	Perseus	Variable Star	2–3	Every 2–3 days Algol drops by nearly a magnitude due to a fainter orbiting companion eclipsing the brighter object.
Albireo	Cygnus	Double star	3	Telescopes show beautiful bluish-purple and yellow double star, excellent color contrast.
γ Andromeda	Andromeda	Double star	2	An orange and blue star form an excellent color contrast, visible in small telescopes.

THE GREEK ALPHABET

LETTER	NAME	LETTER	NAME
α	alpha	ν	nu
β	beta	ξ	xi
γ	gamma	o	omicron
δ	delta	π	pi
ε	epsilon	ρ	rho
ζ	zeta	σ	sigma
η	eta	τ	tau
θ	theta	υ	upsilon
ι	iota	φ	phi
κ	kappa	χ	chi
λ	lambda	ψ	psi
μ	mu	ω	omega

BRIGHTEST STARS

NAME	DESIG.	MAG.	DISTANCE (LY)
Vega	α Lyr	0.0	25
Capella	α Aur	0.1	42
Rigel	β Ori	0.1	773
Betelgeuse	α Ori	0.5	427
Altair	α Aql	0.8	17
Aldebaran	α Tau	0.9	65
Pollux	β Gem	1.1	34
Fomalhaut	α PsA	1.2	25
Deneb	α Cyg	1.3	3,228
Bellatrix	γ Ori	1.6	243
Alnath	β Tau	1.7	131
Alnilan	ε Ori	1.7	1,342

December

The December night sky is dominated by the winter stars rising in the southeastern sky. During this time there are no less than ten first-magnitude stars above the horizon, a dazzling change from just a few months prior. Two of the dazzlers, Vega in the northwest, and Fomalhaut in the southwest, are about to set, to be followed later by Deneb in Cygnus, the Swan.

The other seven bright stars are in the eastern half of the sky. Orion, the Hunter, appears in the southeast. Its two brightest stars, Rigel and Betelgeuse, have dramatically contrasting colors. Rigel is bluish white, while Betelgeuse shines with a distinctly orange hue. These subtle color differences indicate the different surface temperatures of the stars.

The brightest star, Sirius, follows Orion dutifully across the sky like a well-trained dog after its master. Sirius often transmits a wide rainbow of colors—none due to the star itself. Our atmosphere acts like a prism, bending the light from the white star into its component colors. The little dog, Canis Minor, led by the bright star Procyon, performs the same "dog duty" for Gemini, the Twins, found standing high in the eastern sky.

Capturing attention overhead is Perseus. It replaces Cassiopeia, still very high, at the zenith. Perseus is home to the "Demon" star, Algol. Though the star isn't a demon, it performs a peculiar dimming ritual every couple of days or so. Its variations are due to an orbiting fainter star that eclipses its brighter companion.

Lying between Perseus and Orion is the lovely group, Taurus, the Bull, led high in the sky by the Pleiades. This is the finest open cluster in the entire sky. Binoculars show it very well. Aldebaran, the eye of the Bull, marks the tip of a V-shaped group of stars called the Hyades. Less compact than the Pleiades, the Hyades are nonetheless a fine sight in binoculars.

The Beehive Cluster, M44, also known as Praesepe, is just visible to the naked eye between the fourth-magnitude stars Gamma and Delta Cancri. Binoculars reveal nearly 70 stars.

M35, in Gemini, is an easy open cluster for binoculars and visible to the naked eye. Nearby to the right in this image is the cluster NGC 2158.

Due east of Perseus, Auriga, the Charioteer, rides high. Capella, its brightest star, glows with a yellowish hue, easily noticeable when compared to the orange glow from Aldebaran, or Betelgeuse.

The southwestern sky is bland in comparison to the eastern sky. The Square of Pegasus now appears like a giant baseball diamond, suspended above the western horizon. Extending from its upper corner is Andromeda and the large, nearby spiral galaxy M31 remains a pleasing target for observation.

Pisces and Cetus are also descending in the west and southwest. North of Cetus is Aries, essentially three stars forming a crooked line. The brightest of its stars, Hamal, is the same magnitude as Polaris. The faintest of the trio is a fine telescopic double star. Next to Aries is Triangulum; three faint stars form the familiar geometric shape. The large but very faint spiral galaxy M33 lies within its boundaries.

Ursa Major, the Great Bear, is rearing up its huge body in the northeast. The end star of the handle of the Dipper drops below the horizon for many observers. The pair of stars Dubhe and Merak leads the northeasterly ascent.

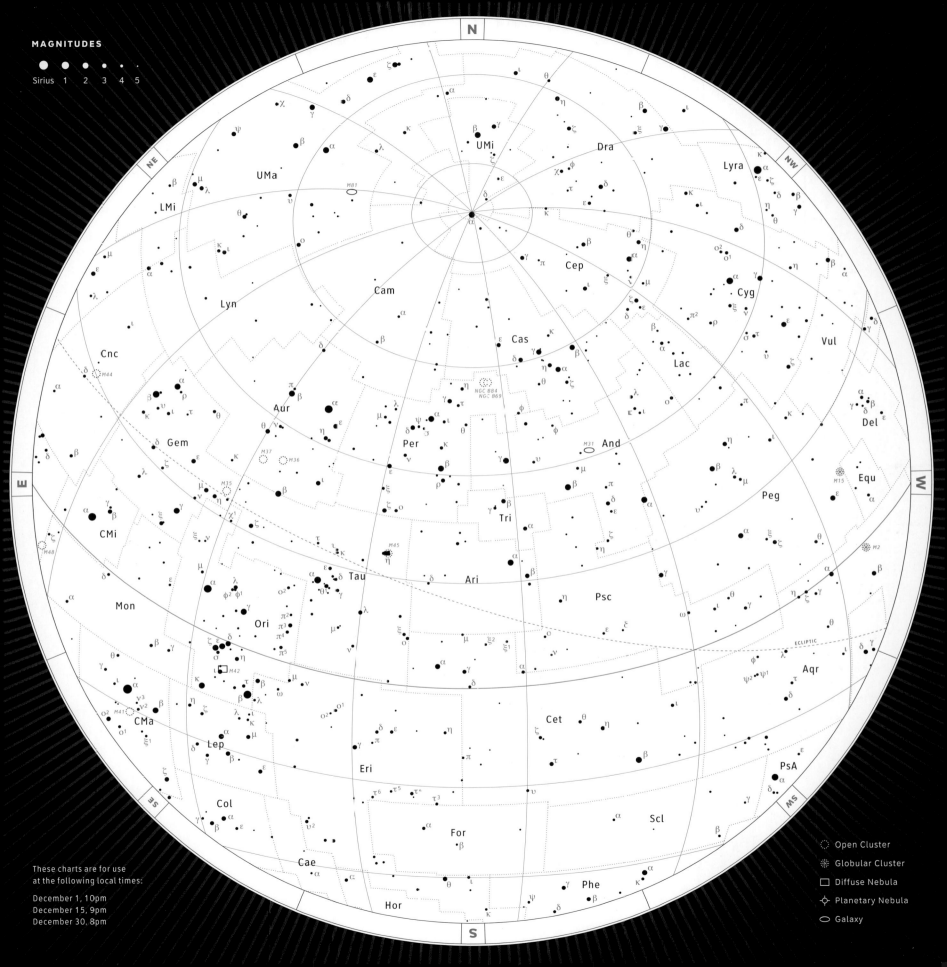

MAGNITUDES

Sirius 1 2 3 4 5

N

NE

NW

UMi

Dra

Lyra

UMa

M81

Cep

Cyg

LMi

Cam

Cas

Vul

Lyn

Lac

Aur

NGC 884
NGC 869

Per

And

M31

Del

Cnc

M44

M37 M36

Equ
M15

E

W

Gem

M35

Tri

Peg

CMi

χ¹

M45

Ari

Psc

M2

ζ

M48

Tau

Mon

Ori

ECLIPTIC

Aqr

ψ² ψ¹

M42

ι

CMa

M41

ν³
ν²
o²

Cet

Lep

Eri

PsA

SE

SW

Col

Scl

For

These charts are for use
at the following local times:

December 1, 10pm
December 15, 9pm
December 30, 8pm

Cae

Phe

Hor

S

⊙ Open Cluster

⊛ Globular Cluster

▢ Diffuse Nebula

◇ Planetary Nebula

◯ Galaxy

December

LIST OF CONSTELLATIONS

NAME	MEANING	ABBREV.
Andromeda	Princess	And
Aquarius	Water Bearer	Aqr
Aries	Ram	Ari
Auriga	Charioteer	Aur
Camelopardalis	Giraffe	Cam
Cancer	Crab	Cnc
Canis Major	Great Dog	CMa
Canis Minor	Little Dog	CMi
Cassiopeia	Queen	Cas
Cepheus	King	Cep
Cetus	Whale	Cet
Cygnus	Swan	Cyg
Delphinus	Dolphin	Del
Draco	Dragon	Dra
Eridanus	River	Eri
Equuleus	Foal	Equ
Fornax	Lab. Furnace	For
Gemini	Twins	Gem
Lacerta	Lizard	Lac
Lepus	Hare	Lep
Lynx	Lynx	Lyn
Lyra	Harp	Lyr
Monoceros	Unicorn	Mon
Orion	Hunter	Ori
Pegasus	Winged Horse	Peg
Perseus	Hero	Per
Pisces	Fish	Psc
Sculptor	Sculpt. Wrkshp.	Scl
Taurus	Bull	Tau
Triangulum	Triangle	Tri
Ursa Minor	Little Bear	UMi
Ursa Major	Great Bear	UMa

DEEP-SKY OBJECTS

These are the brightest of the deep-sky objects greater than magnitude 7 visible on this month's chart and are listed to the nearest whole magnitude. The visibility of deep-sky objects depends on their angular size. Galaxies and nebulae are extended objects and at magnitude 6 may still be difficult to make out because of low surface brightness.

OBJECT	LOCATION	TYPE	MAG.	COMMENTS
NCG 869 & NGC 884	Perseus	Open Cluster	4	The Double Cluster, two fine, rich, open clusters, best seen with binoculars.
M31	Andromeda	Galaxy	4	Andromeda Galaxy, a faint, hazy, elongated cloud, best viewed with binoculars or low-power telescope.
M33	Triangulum	Galaxy	6	An elusive object due to low surface brightness—best viewed in binoculars—very faint.
M35	Gemini	Open Cluster	5	Large open cluster, with 200 stars packed into an area the apparent size of the full moon.
M36	Auriga	Open Cluster	6	M36 and M37 are two fine open clusters visible as fuzzy spots through binoculars and beautiful star clusters when viewed through a small telescope.
M37	Auriga	Open Cluster	6	See M36 notes.
M42	Orion	Nebula	5	The Orion Nebula, the finest star-forming region on view, visible in binoculars as a fuzzy star, and spectacular in any telescope. The central four stars arranged in a trapezoid shape.
M44	Cancer	Open Cluster	3	The Beehive Cluster, also called Praesepe, a fine cluster in binoculars and telescope.
M45	Taurus	Open Cluster	2	The Pleiades, also Seven Sisters, a naked eye object, excellent in binoculars, with nearly 100 stars visible in small telescopes.
Mira	Cetus	Variable Star	3–9	Famous variable star, sometimes naked eye, or faint enough to need binoculars to see it.
Algol	Perseus	Variable Star	2–3	Every 2–3 days Algol drops by nearly a magnitude due to a fainter orbiting companion eclipsing the brighter object.
γ Andromedae	Andromeda	Double star	2	An orange and blue star form an excellent color contrast, visible in small telescopes.

THE GREEK ALPHABET

LETTER	NAME	LETTER	NAME
α	alpha	ν	nu
β	beta	ξ	xi
γ	gamma	o	omicron
δ	delta	π	pi
ε	epsilon	ρ	rho
ζ	zeta	σ	sigma
η	eta	τ	tau
θ	theta	υ	upsilon
ι	iota	φ	phi
κ	kappa	χ	chi
λ	lambda	ψ	psi
μ	mu	ω	omega

BRIGHTEST STARS

NAME	DESIG.	MAG.	DISTANCE (LY)
Sirius	α CMa	−1.5	9
Vega	α Lyr	0.0	25
Capella	α Aur	0.1	42
Rigel	β Ori	0.1	773
Procyon	α CMi	0.4	11
Betelgeuse	α Ori	0.5	427
Aldebaran	α Tau	0.9	65
Pollux	β Gem	1.1	34
Fomalhaut	α PsA	1.2	25
Deneb	α Cyg	1.3	3,228
Bellatrix	γ Ori	1.6	243
Alnath	β Tau	1.7	131

Glossary

Albedo. A measurement of the amount of solar radiation reflected from an object. A pure white object has an albedo of 1.0; a black object has an albedo of 0.0.

Altazimuth. A U-shaped telescope mount allowing movement both up and down (altitude) and left to right (azimuth).

Altitude. The angular distance of a celestial object above the horizon.

Angular diameter. The apparent diameter of a celestial object. For planets this is often expressed in arcseconds (*see* Degree).

Aphelion. The farthest point from the Sun for a planet, comet or asteroid in an elliptical orbit.

Apparent size. The angular diameter of a celestial object as seen from Earth. It's apparent because an object's real size is much larger, and only appears small due to its distance from Earth.

Apogee. The farthest point from the Earth for an object in an elliptical orbit.

Arcminute. One sixtieth of a degree (*see* Degree).

Arcsecond. One sixtieth of an arcminute, which in turn is one sixtieth of a degree (*see* Degree).

Asteroid. Minor planets, most of which orbit the Sun between the orbits of Mars and Jupiter. A few asteroids are in highly elliptical orbits and some cross the orbit of Earth.

Astronomical unit. The average distance of the Earth to the Sun, which is 92.96 million miles. For simplicity, this distance is defined as 1 astronomical unit (a.u.).

Aurora. The northern (borealis) and southern (australis) lights, caused by storms from the Sun energizing particles within Earth's magnetic field. They are usually limited to high latitude areas.

CCD. Charge-coupled device, a type of electronic sensor that is extremely sensitive to light. Used by both professional and amateur astronomers to capture images of celestial objects.

Celestial equator. A giant circle around the celestial sphere that lies directly above the Earth's equator.

Celestial sphere. An imaginary sphere surrounding the Earth with a grid on the sky that matches lines of latitude and longitude.

Cluster. A collection of stars bound by their mutual gravity. An "open cluster" contains several hundred stars, sometimes with associated gas and dust. A globular cluster is spherical in shape, containing many thousands or more stars. Globular clusters are distributed in a spherical halo around a galaxy.

Comet. An object made of ice and rock, typically a few miles across and irregular in shape. Bright comets can generate tails millions of miles long when they approach the Sun.

Conjunction. A line-of-sight alignment of two objects in the sky presenting a small angular separation.

Constellation. A defined region of the sky including a group of stars forming a pattern.

Cosmic microwave background radiation. The very faint microwave radiation left over from the Big Bang discovered in 1965.

Declination. The angular distance of a celestial object north or south of the celestial equator.

Degree. A unit of angular measure (symbol °). A full circle has 360°. The angle from the horizon to the zenith is 90°. The full Moon is 0.5° across. 1° can be divided into 60 segments called arcminutes. Each arcminute can be divided into 60 segments called arcseconds. Also used in measures of temperature.

Double Star. Two stars appearing very close together in the sky. Some are the result of chance alignments, and others, called binary stars, are bound by their mutual gravity, orbiting around each other.

Earthshine. Reflected sunlight off the Earth that shines on the Moon, allowing the Moon's full disk to be seen when it is a thin crescent.

Ecliptic. The plane of the solar system defined by Earth's orbit around the Sun. Also the path of the Sun as seen from Earth projected onto the celestial sphere. Eclipses of the Sun or Moon always occur when both objects are on the ecliptic.

Elongation. The angular distance between the Sun and a planet as seen from Earth.

Equinox. The ecliptic crosses the celestial equator at two points called the equinoxes. The Sun crosses the celestial equator twice a year, on about March 21, the vernal (spring) equinox and September 22, the autumnal (fall) equinox.

Escape Velocity. The minimum velocity an object must move to completely escape the gravitational attraction of a celestial object.

Facula(e). Term used to describe bright areas on the surface of planets, moons, and the Sun.

Galaxy. A collection of billions of stars orbiting around a common center of gravity.

Gibbous. A phase of the Moon or a planet between a half and fully illuminated disk.

Gravity. The force that governs the motion of all objects in the universe. The mutual attraction between two masses.

Inferior planet. Mercury or Venus, the planets orbiting closer to the Sun than the Earth.

Kuiper Belt. A belt of cometary objects orbiting beyond Pluto.

Light year. A unit of measurement equal to the distance a ray of light travels in a vacuum in one year, or approximately 5.88 trillion miles traveling at 186,000 miles per second.

Magnitude. The brightness scale for objects in the night sky.

Meridian. An imaginary vertical line running across the sky from north to south, passing through the zenith (directly overhead).

Messier. French astronomer Charles Messier (June 26, 1730–April 12, 1817) who created the famous Messier catalog of deep-sky objects.

Meteor. A brief flash of light in the sky caused by the burning of a tiny particle entering Earth's atmosphere. Before it reaches the atmosphere, the object is a meteoroid; if it reaches the Earth intact, it's a meteorite.

NGC. New General Catalog, a comprehensive list of over 7,000 galaxies and nebulae, numbered in order of increasing right ascension.

Nebula. A cloud of gas and/or dust, usually associated with new stars. Also known as diffuse nebula and emission nebulae. Plural, nebulae.

Occultation. An event when one celestial object passes behind another and blocks the more distant object from view. The Moon frequently occults stars.

Opposition. When an object in the sky is exactly opposite the Sun relative to the Earth.

Perigee. The nearest point to Earth for an object in an elliptical orbit.

Perihelion. The nearest point to the Sun for a planet, comet or asteroid in an elliptical orbit.

Planet. A non-radiating object in orbit around a star.

Planetary nebula. An expanding gas envelope around a faint star. A planetary nebula is formed when a star is nearing the end of its life.

Precession. The wobble of Earth's polar axis, slowly changing the direction of the poles. One full cycle takes about 26,000 years. Currently, Polaris is the pole star.

Pulsar. A rapidly spinning neutron star with typical periods under 4 seconds. Intense magnetic fields generate beams that flash at the Earth.

Quasar. The brilliant core of an active galaxy that outshines the spiral arms. Energy generated is thought to be from material orbiting a supermassive black hole.

Red Giant. The late stage of a star's life where the outer envelope of the star expands to many times the diameter of the original star.

Retrograde. The apparent backwards motion of an object in the night sky as Earth overtakes it.

Right Ascension. The equivalent of longitude on the celestial sphere.

Satellite. A secondary celestial object orbiting a primary object that orbits a star.

Shooting Star. *See* Meteor.

Sidereal Period. The time taken for a celestial object to orbit the Sun.

Solar Wind. The high-speed wind of energetic particles emitted by the Sun. The solar wind reaches Earth traveling at nearly 500 miles per second.

Solstice. The dates when the Sun reaches its northernmost or southernmost point on the celestial sphere.

Superior planet. The planets that orbit farther from the Sun than Earth. The superior planets are Mars, Jupiter, Saturn, Uranus, and Neptune.

Supernova. A massive stellar explosion. There are two types. Type I involves a white dwarf star in a binary system. Type II is the complete destruction of a massive star and can outshine an entire galaxy.

Variable Star. A star whose output varies over time. The cause can be intrinsic, such as a pulsating star (e.g., Cepheid) or the result of an occultation when the orbit of a binary star is in the plane of our line of sight (e.g., Algol).

White Dwarf. An extremely compact and dense star in a very late stage of its life. A spoonful of white dwarf material would weigh many tons.

Zenith. A point directly over an observer's head.

WEB RESOURCES

There are many web sites where you can explore and learn about the night sky. Here are just a few recommended sites where you can plan a stargazing excursion or simply look at beautiful images.

Adler Planetarium & Astronomy Museum
www.adlerplanetarium.org

Albert Einstein Planetarium
www.nasm.si.edu/visit/planetarium

American Museum of Natural History
Rose Center for Earth and Space
www.amnh.org/rose

Association of Lunar and Planetary Observers (ALPO)
www.lpl.arizona.edu/alpo

Association of Variable Star
Observers (AAVSO)
www.aavso.org

Astronomical Applications Department
U. S. Naval Observatory
http://aa.usno.navy.mil

Astronomical League
www.astroleague.org

Astronomy magazine
www.astronomy.com

Chabot Space & Science Center
www.chabotspace.org

European Space Agency (ESA)
www.esa.int

Hubble Site
www.hubblesite.org

International Dark Sky Association (IDA)
www.darksky.org

International Meteor Organization (IMO)
www.imo.net

International Occultation Timing
Association (IOTA)
www.lunar-occultations.com

Jet Propulsion Laboratory, California
Institute of Technology (JPL-Caltech)
www.jpl.nasa.gov

Museum of Science Boston
Charles Hayden Planetarium
www.mos.org

National Aeronautics
and Space Administration (NASA)
www.nasa.gov

NASA/Goddard Space Flight Center
Eclipse Home Page
http://sunearth.gsfc.nasa.gov/eclipse/eclipse.html

The National Optical
Astronomy Observatory (NOAO)
www.noao.edu/

Planetary Photojournal
http://photojournal.jpl.nasa.gov

Sky and Telescope magazine
www.skytonight.com

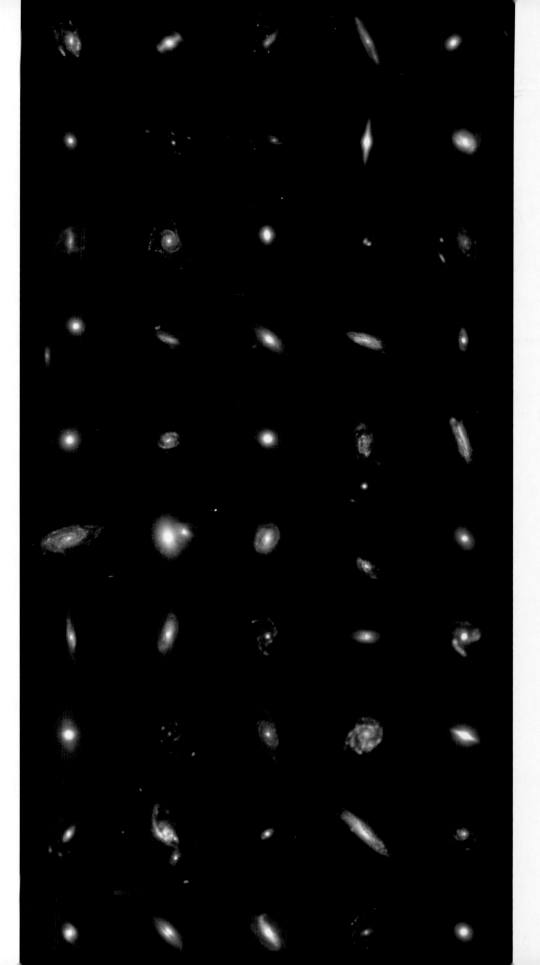

Index